Attachment Theory

for dummies®
A Wiley Brand

Attachment Theory

by Kelley Lockhart Delaune, LCSW

for dummies®
A Wiley Brand

Attachment Theory For Dummies®

Published by: **John Wiley & Sons, Inc.,** 111 River Street, Hoboken, NJ 07030-5774, www.wiley.com

For general information on our other products and services, please contact our Customer Care Department within the U.S. at 877-762-2974, outside the U.S. at 317-572-3993, or fax 317-572-4002. For technical support, please visit https://hub.wiley.com/community/support/dummies.

Wiley publishes in a variety of print and electronic formats and by print-on-demand. Some material included with standard print versions of this book may not be included in e-books or in print-on-demand. If this book refers to media that is not included in the version you purchased, you may download this material at http://booksupport.wiley.com. For more information about Wiley products, visit www.wiley.com.

Library of Congress Control Number is available from the publisher.

ISBN 978-1-394-41068-2 (pbk); ISBN 978-1-394-41071-2 (ebk); ISBN 978-1-394-41070-5 (ebk)

SKY10163060_072026

Contents at a Glance

Table of Contents

Introduction

Have you ever wondered why certain relationships feel effortless, while others leave you anxious, frustrated, or drained? Or why, even as an adult, you still find yourself reacting to loved ones in ways that surprise or confuse you? The answer often lies in something you learned long before you could read a book like this: attachment.

Attachment is the invisible thread that connects us to the people who matter most. It's how we learn what to expect from relationships, how we navigate closeness and distance, how we make friends, how we love romantically, and even how we experience ourselves.

Most people don't struggle with relationships not because they don't care enough. They struggle because they do care, but their nervous systems learned certain rules about closeness long before they had words for them.

The good news is that attachment patterns aren't fixed. They're learned strategies that are built in early in life and reinforced over time, but with awareness, reflection, and practice, you can change them. You can understand why you feel what you feel and then act in ways that feel more intentional and create healthier, more fulfilling relationships.

Attachment theory helps explain why some relationships feel steady and safe, whereas others leave you anxious, shut down, or stuck in the same patterns.

About This Book

Attachment theory can sound complicated or overly clinical, but at its core, it's about something deeply human: how people connect, how you protect yourself when connection feels risky, and how those patterns from childhood follow you into adulthood. This book is designed to help you recognize those patterns in everyday life and understand what to do with them.

In this book, I guide you through:

- Recognizing where attachment shows up in family, friendships, and romantic relationships
- Understanding your own attachment patterns, including what feels comfortable, what triggers cause worry or distance, and why you feel those things
- Acquiring practical strategies to move toward secure attachment by building awareness, developing emotional regulation, discovering coping strategies, and working on communication skills

Whether you're reading this to better understand yourself, your family, or your relationships, you're in the right place. Attachment theory may sound like psychology jargon, but in practice, it's really about something you've been navigating your whole life: connection.

This book is organized to help you recognize attachment where it actually shows up in adult life. You find out:

- What attachment is and how it forms
- Why romantic relationships tend to activate attachment most strongly
- How attachment patterns show up in relationships with parents even in adulthood
- How attachment influences friendships, especially under stress or during life transitions
- How people develop earned secure attachment over time

If you choose to move through the book in order, each section builds on the last, moving from awareness to understanding to possibility.

Foolish Assumptions

You don't need a psychology background to read this book. You don't need to remember every detail of your childhood. And you don't need to fit neatly into a single attachment "style." Attachment shows up differently depending on the relationship, the season of life you're in, and the amount of stress you're carrying. This book honors that complexity.

As I was writing this book, I made a few foolish assumptions about you:

- You're curious about attachment.
- You may have heard words like *secure*, *avoidant*, or *anxious*.
- You want to know the origins of attachment theory and how it came about so that you can better understand it.
- You want to be able to recognize how attachment shows up in your life.
- You want to know what tools will help you to navigate attachment and relationships better.

This book is:

- A user-friendly introduction to attachment theory
- Grounded in real-life examples
- Focused on awareness
- Written with compassion for both you and the people you're attached to

This book is not:

- About blaming parents or rewriting your childhood
- A substitute for therapy (though many people may find it helpful alongside therapy)

Icons Used in This Book

Throughout this book, icons in the margins highlight certain types of valuable information that call out for your attention. Here are the icons you'll encounter and a brief description of each.

TIP

Tips are practical suggestions and strategies you can use to strengthen relationships.

REMEMBER

The Remember icon tells you that what's coming are key takeaways, important concepts, and foundational ideas worth keeping in mind as you move through the book.

TECHNICAL STUFF

If you want a deeper dive into the research, science, and theory behind attachment, relationships, and behavior, pay attention to the text marked with the Technical Stuff icon.

WARNING

Common pitfalls, attachment patterns, and misunderstandings that can get in the way are flagged with the Warning icon.

EXAMPLE

Examples are real-world illustrations that show how attachment concepts play out in friendships, family relationships, dating, and romantic partnerships.

Beyond the Book

In addition to the abundance of information and guidance related to attachment theory that I provide in this book, you get access to even more help and information online at `Dummies.com`. Check out this book's online Cheat Sheet. Just go to `www.dummies.com` and search for "Attachment Theory For Dummies Cheat Sheet." On the Cheat Sheet, you'll find out how to recognize common attachment styles and how to respond more effectively when attachment fears and emotional triggers arise. The Cheat Sheet also covers strategies for taking productive time-outs during conflict, turning toward your partner instead of away, repairing relationship ruptures, and staying grounded during difficult conversations. You can also find guidance for navigating the dating world through an attachment lens, identifying signs of a more secure partner, and creating regular relationship practices that help strengthen connection over time.

Where to Go from Here

As with all dummies books, you don't have to read this book straight through. Some readers start with the sections that feel most relevant right now. Others read from beginning to end to see the full picture.

As you read, you may experience moments of recognition, discomfort, or relief. That's normal. Attachment awareness often brings clarity before it brings change. You don't need to fix anything as you go. Just notice.

If you find yourself thinking, *This sounds like me* or *This sounds like someone I love*, you're using the book exactly as intended.

1 The Basics of Attachment

IN THIS PART . . .

Understand what's happening with your feelings underneath the surface so you can change the way you show up in relationships.

Find out what attachment is and how it shapes how you connect with others, how you handle closeness, how you respond to distance, and what you do when something feels off in a relationship.

Get a clear picture of what's happening in your nervous system when your attachment responses are triggered so you can begin to respond in ways that feel more steady, intentional, and aligned with the kind of relationships you want.

IN THIS CHAPTER

» Understanding why attachment matters

» Exploring the research

» Tracing the origins of attachment patterns

Chapter 1 Understanding Attachment

Exploring the world of attachment requires entering into a framework that deeply values relationships. Attachment theory focuses on people's need to forge bonds with their caregivers from the moment of birth, and it continues to impact attachments in any other relationships through a person's lifetime.

Attachment theory attends to the physiological and psychological processes that shape how people connect. It provides a perspective that recognizes closeness, independence, safety, and vulnerability. Everything in attachment is dynamic and always shifting, yet the need to connect is constant. The path toward relational health starts with noticing and accepting how these forces show up in ourselves and others. This chapter introduces attachment and why it matters in our lives and relationships.

Taking Attachment Seriously

There are good reasons to take attachment theory seriously. Why does it matter?

» Attachment shapes your entire relational world. Attachment isn't just a childhood concept; it's the blueprint through which you interpret people and safety.

It influences how you read facial expressions, tones, and intentions. It shapes how much trust you extend and how quickly you pull away or confidently you move toward others. It affects your capacity for intimacy, independence, and repair after conflict.

REMEMBER

- **»** Attachment is not just feelings; its biological. Attachment lives in the nervous system. It's built into the brain and your body's response patterns. The attachment system is tied to survival instincts, seeking closeness, coregulation, and protection. Hormones like oxytocin, cortisol, and adrenaline work with attachment needs.

WARNING

Ignoring attachment has real consequences such as:

- **» Difficulty regulating emotions:** Difficulty calming down, staying grounded, or tolerating discomfort
- **» Recurring relational conflict:** Misreading partner's intentions, escalating protest behaviors, avoidance, or repeated rupture cycles
- **» Repeated patterns of hurt:** Choosing familiar but unhealthy dynamics, reenacting unresolved attachment injuries, or getting stuck in the same relational scripts

Attachment can also have an impact on our mental and physical health, resulting in chronic stress, inflammation, anxiety, depression, and sleep disturbances because the nervous system never truly rests when attachment system feels threatened.

TIP

When you take attachment seriously, you can pay attention and increase your awareness:

- **»** You can become intentional about slowing down and noticing the patterns in your relationships. You can notice what you reach for, what you avoid, and what you fear.
- **»** You not only notice your own attachment system but can also begin to notice and understand the attachment system of your friends, family members, and loved ones.

Researching the Research

To understand the details of attachment, it helps to understand how attachment theory developed. It didn't appear out of thin air but came from decades of observations and experiments developed by studying people across infancy, adolescence, and adulthood. This section walks you through the foundational research so you can see why attachment matters for survival and how it develops across different stages of life.

Why attachment is essential for survival

John Bowlby was a British psychiatrist and psychoanalyst who radically shifted how the world understood human development. Before Bowlby, mainstream psychology assumed children were mainly motivated by food, reward, and conditioning. Bowlby challenged that position by arguing that children are driven by the need for emotional connection and protection. He was interested in the distress that babies felt when they were separated from their caregivers. Bowlby observed that when children were scared, they wanted to be close to their caregivers.

Here are the Pillars of Bowlby's work:

» **Attachment is a survival system.** Bowlby argued that humans are born with an innate system designed to keep us alive. Long before infants can walk or talk, they're wired to seek warmth and safety through crying, reaching for, and tracking their caregivers.

» **Early relationships shape internal working models.** Bowlby proposed that our earliest relational experiences become the blueprint for how we understand ourselves and others. Working models are formed from how we were held, responded to, soothed, or ignored. Bowlby suggested that a child's early attachment creates a template that guides their expectations and the way they show up in future relationships.

Over time, these repeated experiences with caregivers shape a child's internal working model, deeply held beliefs about themselves, other people, and what they can expect from relationships, as described here:

- **When caregivers are consistently attuned,** a child's nervous system learns, "my needs matter. People can be trusted." This creates an internal working model that supports secure attachment. Read more about secure attachment in Chapter 4.
- **When caregiving is inconsistent, intrusive, unpredictable, or emotionally unavailable,** a child's working model might sound like, "I need to cling to stay safe," "I shouldn't need anyone," or "Closeness is risky."

» **Separation and loss matter deeply.** Bowlby took his observations and theories and applied them to grief. Bowlby identified a pattern in the way children responded to separation from their caregivers. He described three phases:

- **Protest:** When a child is first separated from their caregiver, they cling, cry, and have an immediate intense reaction. He found that protest is the initial reaction to loss.
- **Despair:** Despair happens when the caregiver does not return and the child becomes withdrawn and sad.
- **Detachment:** This last stage is where the child emotionally detaches.

These reactions to separation can later influence the way attachment patterns show up.

» **A secure base gives a child safety.** In Bowlby's work, a secure base is a caregiver who provides security and consistency so that the child can feel confident to go explore the world and return.

Categorizing attachments in infants

Developmental psychologist Mary Ainsworth took Bowlby's ideas and turned them into something people could visualize. Ainsworth and her colleague Sylvia Bell created a research procedure called The Strange Situation, which was a short play session that followed this structure:

1. A caregiver and baby enter a room.
2. The baby plays.
3. A stranger enters.
4. The caregiver leaves.
5. The caregiver returns.

In the study, about 100 one- to two-year-olds and their mothers came into a playroom filled with toys. The setup was designed to feel novel enough that the children would explore but not so unfamiliar that they would immediately panic.

Over the course of 20 minutes, the mother and a friendly stranger took turns entering and leaving the room while the baby played. Researchers carefully watched for the following things:

» How the baby explored

» How upset they became when the mother left

» How they behaved when she returned

» How they interacted with the stranger

Patterns were revealed about how babies look to their caregivers for comfort and safety. From these patterns, Ainsworth identified different attachment styles, which became the foundation of modern attachment theory.

Ainsworth's three attachment patterns

Ainsworth identified three primary attachment patterns:

» **Secure attachment:** Ainsworth observed that with this form of attachment, the baby was upset when the caregiver left but was comforted easily when they returned. The baby uses the caregiver as the base, checking in but also exploring.

» **Anxious ambivalent attachment:** With this form of attachment, the baby displayed high levels of distress when the caregiver left, but they weren't comforted by their return. They also were wary of the stranger and didn't show as much exploration behavior.

» **Anxious avoidant attachment:** In this case, the baby appeared unbothered when the caregiver left and also avoided or ignored the caregiver upon their return. These babies were stressed physiologically, but they don't show it.

The importance of Ainsworth's work for adults

REMEMBER

Even though Ainsworth did her research with infants, the categories became the foundation for modern adult attachment theory. These early strategies for getting connection, protest behaviors for anxious attachment, and shutting down for avoidant attachment show up later in adult relationships, especially during conflict.

Attachment in adolescents

Joseph P. Allen and Joseph Tan's work focuses on what happens to attachment as children move into adolescence, a stage where everything shifts in the brain, body, social life, and, of course, relationships with caregivers.

The core concepts of Allen and Tan's work include these ideas:

» **Adolescence reshapes attachment.** Teens don't outgrow attachment. They reorganize it. Where young children rely directly on caregivers for comfort and coregulation, adolescents begin shifting that dependence from parents to peers. Attachment needs for safety, acceptance, and attunement remain the same.

» **Teens still need a secure base.** Allan and Tan emphasize that secure attachment in adolescence looks like:

- A teen who feels they can explore their world but still return home for support
- A parent who stays available, responsive, and nonreactive even when the teen pushes back
- A parent who provides emotional scaffolding rather than control

What is emotional scaffolding?

Emotional scaffolding involves guiding a teen's emotional development by providing support and a secure base while gradually letting them develop autonomy. Control is more of an authoritative approach that can hinder teens in developing independence.

Emotional scaffolding is guiding, validation, intimacy, dialogue, coaching, debriefing, and staying attuned and consistent. Control is invalidation, dominance, and micromanaging. Research shows that high levels of control are linked to negative impacts.

Threats to the attachment system look different at various ages. In infancy, a threat shows up as crying, clinging, or shutting down. In adolescence, the same attachment system exists, but it's expressed with teen versions of these behaviors. In adolescents, protest behaviors might look like:

» Emotional flooding is feeling so overwhelmed that it becomes difficult to think clearly, stay present, or communicate effectively. It can show up in the following ways:

- People pleasing
- Jealousy
- Fear of abandonment
- "Do you even care?" testing behaviors

In adolescents, avoidant behaviors may look like:

- Pulling away
- Saying, "I'm fine" instead of sharing emotions or experiences
- Overindependence
- Minimizing emotions

In adolescence, peer relationships become part of the attachment system. For securely attached teens, this development creates healthy autonomy and supportive friendships.

However, for insecurely attached teens, peer relationships can become:

- **Overly fused (often linked to anxious attachment):** Some insecurely attached teens become intensely dependent on friendships or romantic relationships. They may fear rejection, struggle with boundaries, or feel anxious when there is distance or conflict.
- **Highly conflictual (can occur in insecure or disorganized attachment patterns):** Other teens may experience relationships as emotionally volatile, moving quickly between closeness and anger, reassurance seeking, withdrawal or emotional outbursts.
- **Distant or dismissive (often linked to avoidant attachment):** Some teens protect themselves by minimizing emotional needs, avoiding vulnerability, or keeping others at arm's length.

REMEMBER

This shift from attachment to caregivers to attachment to peers is one of the most important developmental tasks of adolescence.

Despite the shift to attachment to peers, parent regulation still predicts teen regulation. Allen and Tan's work found that teens still look to their parents for help with regulation, even though they may be more independent. The parents' nervous system still impacts the adolescent and can assist a teen through:

- Modeling
- Remaining calm under stress
- Providing healthy boundaries
- Assisting with repair after conflict

The VIDA Project: Shedding light on teen attachment

TECHNICAL STUFF

In 1998, the VIDA Project followed 184 adolescents for more than a decade to understand how attachment develops and how it shapes later relationships. Here are some of the key findings from that research:

- Early adolescent attachment security predicts later romantic competence. Teens who were more secure communicated better and handled conflict better.
- Insecure attachment predicts behavioral and emotional difficulties.
- Secure teens function better with peers. They showed stronger peer competence and were less vulnerable to negative peer pressure.

REMEMBER

The bottom line from this project is that adolescent attachment is a major developmental pathway that shapes relationships in adulthood.

Applying attachment theory to adult romantic relationships

Cindy Hazen and Phillip Shaver extended Bowlby and Ainsworth's attachment framework beyond intimacy and childhood to show that romantic relationships function as attachment bonds. Their work was foundational in shifting the field toward understanding adult love through the attachment lens.

Here are the key contributions from Hazen and Shaver's work:

- **Adult romantic partners serve the same attachment functions as caregivers.** Haxen and Shaver proposed that romantic partners act as:
  - Safe havens
  - Secure bases
  - Figures of proximity
  - Figures whose loss causes distress

  REMEMBER

  Attachment is not just for children!
- **Adult attachment styles mirror infant attachment patterns.** Hazen and Shaver argued that the attachment styles observed by Ainsworth appear again in adulthood as:

- Secure
- Anxious
- Avoidant

» **Early experiences shape later romantic expectations.** Drawing on Bowlby's work, Hazen and Shaver showed that internal working models formed early in life guide how adults:

- Perceive partner availability
- Interpret conflict
- Regulate emotion
- Seek or withdraw closeness

The disorganized attachment style

The fourth attachment pattern, disorganized attachment, was identified by Mary Main and Judith Solomon in the late 1980s when they noticed a subset of infants in the Strange Situation Study did not fit the existing secure, avoidant, or anxious types. These children showed contradictory, confused, or frozen behaviors when seeking comfort.

At the heart of disorganized attachment is a fundamental conflict: The caregiver is the source of comfort *and* fear. Disorganized attachment style is a combination of anxious and avoidant behaviors, leading to a push-pull dynamic. Read more about disorganized attachment in Chapter 7.

Where Do Attachment Styles Come From?

Where do our attachment styles come from? John Bowlby, a pioneer in attachment theory, believed they grow out of a person's lived experiences, especially the interactions they have with their caregivers in infancy. But research now shows that attachment isn't the product of just one source.

For example, newer research indicates that genes can also play an important role in attachment styles. One study by Leslie Atkinson (2000), which drew data from more than 2,000 parent/child pairs, found a weak but meaningful link between sensitive caregiving and secure attachment. The reason the connection wasn't stronger was because other factors also shape attachment, such as a child's temperament, a parent's mental health, social support, and even the amount of non-parental childcare.

REMEMBER

Attachment styles aren't fixed. There is increasing evidence that a person's attachment styles can shift over time, and adult romantic relationships can strengthen someone's sense of security or, in some cases, make us feel less safe in close relationships.

Understanding these core ideas gives you a roadmap for recognizing your own patterns and offers a hopeful starting point for building more secure, grounded connections moving forward.

IN THIS CHAPTER

» Dispelling common attachment theory myths

» Focusing on the true nature of attachment

» Seeing attachment as the key to regulating emotions

» Recognizing the dynamic nature of attachment

Chapter 2 Defining What Attachment Is (and Isn't)

In today's world, *attachment* has become a buzzword in parenting books, relationship podcasts, and on social media. Social media alone has helped to make attachment theory mainstream. These days, attachment isn't just a topic for therapists. It's showing up in everyday conversations from Generation x and Millennials — even all the way to Gen Alpha teens. In the last 20 years, there has been a cultural shift toward emotional awareness, so it makes sense that attachment theory has gained visibility. As a clinician, I love seeing attachment getting the attention it deserves. With that said, along with the attention comes some misconceptions. In this chapter, I clarify what attachment is — and what it isn't.

Carving Out What Attachment Isn't

Attachment is often oversimplified, which can lead to confusion. That's why it's important to pause and clarify what attachment really is and what it isn't. I'll start by clearing up some of the most common myths about attachment, so you can approach it with clarity and compassion.

Attachment isn't good or bad

One of the common misconceptions is the idea that a certain attachment style is good or bad. For example, many people come to believe that it's negative to be *avoidant* or *anxious*. (For more on the specific attachment styles, see Chapters 4, 5, 6, and 7.) In reality, attachment explains how a person learned to relate to others. Understanding attachment isn't about labeling; it's about understanding patterns so that you can adjust if those patterns are no longer working for you or your relationships.

EXAMPLE

Paige lost both of her parents at an early age to alcoholism. She has worked hard to build a life for herself with resources and support. She went to college and built a thriving business.

In relationships, when Paige feels hurt by someone, it triggers deep feelings of sadness and fear. She copes with this by requesting reassurance from her partner or loved one. Reassurance helps her to feel emotionally safe and secure.

Paige met Brad through a mutual friend, and they immediately had a strong connection and they've been together for a year.

Brad grew up in a family with inconsistent caregivers. In some ways, his caregivers were safe, loving, and nurturing. Like Paige, he too had alcoholism in his family of origin, and this often caused chaos and fear. Brad learned to deal with this by suppressing his feelings.

As Paige and Brad grew closer and moved past the romantic phase, conflicts started to arise. Paige's anxious attachment style caused her to want frequent reassurance. Brad's avoidant style caused him to need more space.

Neither style is wrong. They're just different. Paige and Brad have similar feelings during times of stress, yet they have different needs. They operate from different survival strategies that they developed in their families of origin.

Attachment styles aren't permanent

Our attachment styles aren't solid or fixed. In the therapy office and even out in the wild, it's common to hear someone say, "But I'm an avoidant or I'm anxious." Although it's wonderful that many people now know what their attachment style is, it's important that you're careful about how you frame this.

REMEMBER

Attachment style isn't permanent. You can shift, change, and adjust your style as you grow and learn. You can move from being secure to being anxious or from being anxious to avoidant. You can also go from a secure attachment style to avoidant or disorganized. This is because your experiences impact your attachment styles. Even though your attachment styles form early, they can change when you have secure experiences or you have inconsistencies or trauma.

REMEMBER

Attachment can change through the following mechanisms:

- **Awareness and understanding:** As you increase your awareness of your attachment styles and what you're feeling, you can develop new ways of regulating your emotions.
- **Practice:** As you practice new coping strategies such as grounding yourself — breathing, mindfulness, or processing your emotions in healthy ways — hour attachment style can shift.
- **Supportive relationships:** Supportive, secure relationships can gradually shift attachment styles. Consistent experiences of being seen, heard, and cared for can retrain your nervous system.
- **Corrective experiences:** A corrective experience is when you have opportunity to correct old beliefs or relational habits that came from previous negative experiences.
- **Therapy:** Couples therapy and individual therapy can help you to rewire your nervous system and relational patterns. It can also help you develop new coping strategies. See Chapter 18 for information on working with a therapist.
- **Loss or grief:** When you lose someone through death, betrayal, divorce, or even a breakup, your attachment system is deeply triggered. Your attachment style can change as your basic trust or sense of safety is lost. In my practice as a clinician, I've seen countless people shift to a more anxious attachment style during the grief process. Research by Antje Janshen and colleagues (2024) show that anxious and avoidant attachment styles were positively correlated with prolonged grief symptoms. However, it's important to note that as painful as loss is, individuals can also become more secure when others respond to them with empathy, understanding, and presence.

Attachment isn't just about your childhood

Attachment isn't just about your childhood. It starts in your childhood, but it extends to adolescence, young adulthood, and beyond.

Attachment styles can help to explain how you respond to different challenges, such as uncertainty, conflict, and expectations within a relationship. The patterns that you develop in childhood continue to show up in your adolescent and adult relationships. Furthermore, your adult relationships can reactivate old wounds or help you to rewire your nervous systems through safe experiences.

EXAMPLE

Michael grew up in a household where there was silence for days after a conflict. Now, when he and his wife have conflict, Michael shuts down completely. Michael developed avoidant attachment style.

Zeroing In on What Attachment Is

At its most basic level, attachment describes your emotional bond with people that you care about. Here are some qualities to understand about attachment:

- It's relational.
- It affects how you handle closeness and distance.
- It can change.
- It's fluid and ever evolving.

Seeing attachment as part of a biological system

From the moment you're born, you're completely reliant on your caregivers for your basic needs. You reach out and cry when you need food, warmth, or affection. Your nervous system becomes attuned to ensuring your survival and seeks to soothe itself through connecting with another person. When that connection feels secure, your bod relaxes, and your heart rate slows. When your bond feels threatened through distance, your system shifts into fear or anxiety. Attachment is biological.

As an adult, this same biology is at play, only now it shows up with your friends and lovers.

Consider the study done by Dr. James Coan and colleagues. He gave MRI scan to married women. Some of the women took the scan alone, others had the scan while holding a stranger's hand and the last group were given the scan while holding their husband's hand. During the scan, the doctor told the women that they would receive a mild electrical shock. In a stressful situation, our hippocampus typically lights up. The results showed that the hippocampus of the women who were alone lit up. There was mild activation in the women who were holding a stranger's hand. The women who were holding their life partner's hands showed hardly any detectable signs of stress. This study demonstrates the power of attachment. It is not only emotional. It is physiological.

REMEMBER

Close relationships can help you to regulate your emotions. Connection feels calming, and distance can feel destabilizing. This is biology at work.

Understanding the complexity of attachment

Attachment is complex. The same childhood experience can wire two different people in completely different ways. As a clinician, I often see siblings who were raised in the same home by the same caregivers who have different attachment styles.

EXAMPLE

In Tammy's childhood, after conflict, there was silence for days. In her adult relationship with her husband Joe, when they have conflict, Tammy shuts down for 24 hours. Tammy had caregivers with avoidant attachment style, and she developed an avoidant attachment style.

EXAMPLE

Mary grew up in a home, like Tammy, where her caregiver shut down. After conflict, her mother would experience overwhelming emotions and shut herself in her bedroom to self-soothe.

In her adult relationships, Mary was anxious. She would move toward her partners during conflict, reaching for security. Mary had parents with an avoidant attachment style, and Mary developed an anxious attachment style.

EXAMPLE

Jason also grew up in a home with caregivers who shut down during conflict, but he had one parent who was somewhat available during conflict. Jason developed a disorganized attachment style. When Jason has conflict with his partner, his reactions are unpredictable. While Jason wants closeness, he often sabotages or pushes his partner away.

Stressing the importance of attachment as a relational bond

In the complexity of human relationships, attachment can sometimes be confused as dependency, but the two are not the same. You're probably familiar with the language of romantic love, the butterflies, and the intense feelings that you can have in the beginning of a relationship. This is chemistry. Chemistry has a pull that that draws you toward someone; it's similar to the pull that you felt toward your caregivers when you were young.

REMEMBER

Our desire to be relational is natural. However, as most people move into adulthood, we start to get mixed messages about independence and dependence. We are told, "Be independent. You don't need another person to make you happy," as if relying on another person makes you weak. Society values independence, and yet the science of attachment tells us that we're wired for connection. So, which is the truth?

The truth is somewhere in the middle: interdependence.

Interdependence is the idea that we have our own lives while also relying on each other for support. An interdependent relationship allows us to maintain our uniqueness, our interests, our friendships, and our beliefs while also joining with a partner for love, partnership, support, and companionship.

EXAMPLE

Jane is in a relationship with Carlos. Jane gets frustrated when Carlos goes out with his friends. He goes out to play pool about twice a month. There are no previous trust issues in the relationship. Jane had a caregiver who was inconsistent and mostly emotionally unavailable. She witnessed her father having multiple affairs, which was traumatic for her. Jane lived in a state of hypervigilance and constantly feared being left in her childhood. Jane has anxious attachment style. She panics when Carlos goes on these outings with his buddies. It feels like a threat to her attachment system.

Part of my work in therapy with Jane was working on interdependence. One of the concepts that we regularly discussed was the I, the you, and the we.

Therapist Terry Real teaches that every relationship is built on three entities:

- The "I" is your individual self.
- The "you" is respect for your partner's experience.
- The "we" is the shared relationship.

According to Brene Brown, people are wired for connection. It's central to why we exist and what makes life fulfilling. It is in our safe, intimate relationships that we're able to feel secure enough to explore the world. Researcher Mary Ainsworth referred to this as the *secure base*. (Read more about Mary Ainsworth's work in Chapter 1.) When infants have a secure base, they can leave their caregivers and feel safe enough to venture out and return. This is also true for adults. When we have a safe partnership, we can go out and explore careers, interests, and friendships and know that we have a secure base at home.

All Systems Go: Recognizing Attachment as a System for Emotional Regulation

As a clinician, I see varying capacities for emotional regulation in the therapy room. How people regulate their emotions has a major impact on their relationships with themselves and others.

At its core, *emotional regulation* refers to how you notice, manage, and respond to your feelings. It's a multistep process that includes recognizing your internal experience, calming your body's reaction, and choosing actions that reflect your values instead of your impulses. There are many strategies that help turn down the volume on overwhelming emotions.

This section explores how emotional regulation is shaped by attachment. Attachment is the brain's built-in blueprint for how to calm yourself down and feel safe. Early experiences with caregivers teach children what to do when they're distressed. When caregivers are mostly attuned and responsive, they model healthy ways of coping. This helps a child feel secure in themself and in the world, sending the message *I can handle big feelings. When I need support, someone will show up for me.* Over time, children internalize this sense of safety and learn how to regulate emotions like anger, sadness, and fear.

Secure attachment teaches the following things:

- Feelings are safe to have.
- Comfort is available when I need it.
- I can survive difficult emotions and return to balance.

When a child's caregivers are inconsistent or unavailable, this often leads to challenges with regulating emotions. Responsiveness to your own feelings as well as the way you respond to the feelings of your loved ones is shaped by what was modeled for you.

REMEMBER

Even for parents who deeply love their children, lots of factors can contribute to their inability to provide a base of secure attachment, which in turn impacts emotional regulation. Here are some examples:

- **Lack of understanding of the importance of attachment:** Our understanding of attachment is still relatively new in the grand scheme of parenting knowledge. Many older generations simply didn't have access to what we now know about how secure relationships shape emotional health. Even today, despite growing awareness, it's easy to overlook or minimize the importance of attachment, especially when a parent is stretched thin, stressed, and trying to keep up with the Joneses or the pace of modern life. We live in a culture that prioritizes productivity and independence, so slowing down to be more emotionally attuned can get lost or pushed to the wayside.
- **Outdated beliefs about parenting:** Even today, many common ideas about parenting can conflict with the principles of attachment. Beliefs such as "responding to them immediately will spoil them" or "We need to toughen

them up" are still common things we hear. These messages are dismissive of feelings. They can teach children that their feelings are inconvenient or a sign of weakness. While I understand the importance of allowing a child to work through their feelings, it's equally important that you respond in a way that shows them how to navigate difficult emotions. Responding to a child's stress doesn't remove the feeling; it helps them learn to tolerate and manage it safely.

- **The controlling/hovering parent:** Caregivers who are controlling, overinvolved, or hovering are on the other extreme of the continuum. Their approach can be overresponsive, which can also undermine secure attachment because children aren't learning self-regulation or independence. Examples include micromanaging every decision or intervening before a child can try something on their own.

- **Substance misuse:** According to the National Institutes of Health, one in four children in the United States lives in a home with at least one parent with a substance use disorder. The NIH also reports that 46 million adults had a substance use disorder in 2023. Substance misuse affects entire families, and it can significantly disrupt attachment styles for everyone in the household. The chaos, fear, and instability that often accompany substance misuse create inconsistent caregiving and model destructive coping strategies. This makes it difficult for children and even other adults in the home to regulate their emotions.

- **Untreated mental health issues:** Struggles with untreated mental health conditions such as depression, anxiety, or PTSD can significantly affect a caregiver's ability to respond to a child's needs. These challenges can impact mood, increase irritability, or make a caregiver less emotionally available. They can interfere with a parent's ability to stay connected or be consistent with nurturing interactions. Like substance misuse, untreated mental health issues can make it harder for caregivers to be reliably present, which can disrupt a child's sense of safety and the development of secure attachment.

- **Trauma:** Parents who have experienced trauma, whether in childhood or adulthood, may struggle with regulating their own emotions. When someone experiences trauma, their nervous system often remains alert, making it harder to regulate emotions and respond with calm consistency. This can lead to hypervigilance, withdrawal, or reactivity that disrupts the steady, predictable connection.

REMEMBER

When a caregiver is emotionally unavailable, inconsistent, or only attuned under certain conditions, children learn that their internal experiences are either not seen or not safe to express. This directly affects a child's capacity to regulate emotions because regulation begins externally: A caregiver helps a child make sense of their feelings by labeling them, soothing them, or staying present with

them. If that support is missing or unpredictable, the child's nervous system doesn't get reliable coregulation. (Coregulation is essentially the way that another person helps you to regulate your emotions by being present.) A parent rocking a crying baby is coregulation. A parent of a teen simply listening to the teen's fears with loving presence is coregulation. In an adult partnership, touching your partner's shoulder when they're are crying is coregulation.

Consider the Still Face experiment conducted by Dr. Edward Tronick. In the experiment, a caregiver interacts normally with an infant and then suddenly becomes still and unresponsive. The baby's responses are observed during this "still face" period. When the caregiver became still faced, the baby would become distressed as evidenced by physiological changes such as increased heart rate. This gives us information about what happens when connection doesn't occur. When the caregiver behaves differently, the baby can't regulate because the infant's ability to regulate emotions is highly dependent on the caregiver. In the experiment, the caregiver later returned to the distressed infant and soothed them. As you might imagine, the infants eventually calmed down with their caregiver's soothing responsiveness.

EXAMPLE

Shawna's mom Brenda was present at all of her softball games, as well as at every school event. She showed Shawna that she was proud of her by affirming her hard work in athletics and academics. When Shawna was sad or distressed, Brenda would become anxious, and she would shut down. She couldn't listen to Shawna's fears or help Shawna to calm down. Shawna's mom Brenda was raised by parents who didn't have the capacity to be with their emotions or her emotions. Brenda never learned how to tolerate strong emotions and therefore, she wasn't able to help Shawna to regulate her own emotions.

Delving into the Dynamic Nature of Attachment

Attachment style is relational. Our patterns both influence and are influenced by the way we connect with others. Different partners, different histories, and different relational patterns can activate different parts of us. An anxiously attached person might soften with a responsive partner, or a typically secure person may feel more avoidant if they've been dismissed.

EXAMPLE

Riley grew up feeling mostly secure. Friends liked Riley, and her parents were mostly present. Then Riley started dating Megan. Megan was charming, but sometimes Megan would disappear for hours and ignore Riley's text messages. Megan changed plans at the last minute and told Riley she was too sensitive whenever Riley had complaints. Suddenly Riley changed. She went from secure to checking her phone constantly and wondering what she'd done wrong. Riely's secure attachment shifted to an anxious style in this relationship with Megan.

EXAMPLE

Sam grew up with caregivers who were sometimes loving and sometimes scary. Comfort and fear got all tangled up for Sam. As an adult, Sam developed a disorganized attachment style. Part of Sam wants closeness, and part of Sam fears closeness. Sam met Alicia. Alicia was patient, predictable and emotionally steady. Sam learned that closeness could feel safe. After his relationship with Alicia, Sam met Jessica. With Jessica, love was intense and up and down. Jessica disappeared for some days and wanted distance. Sam's nervous system shifted back to the way it had been in childhood. Sam developed a push-pull dynamic with Jessica. Some days he ghosted her and some days he wanted to connect.

IN THIS CHAPTER

» **Examining the nervous system as a whole**

» **Understanding an activated nervous system**

Chapter 3 Understanding Attachment and the Nervous System

Attachment is connected to regulating emotions. Long before you had words to describe how you feel, your nervous system would scan for safety, attunement, and connection. You relied on tiny connections from your caregivers to guide your nervous system. Your early life experiences shape your limbic system, the parts of your brain and body that manage emotion, memory, and stress response. When children experience secure attachment, these systems strengthen the parts of the brain that help them calm down after stress. But if a person doesn't feel safety consistently early on, their nervous system can become wired to expect stress instead of calm.

This chapter looks at how the nervous system and attachment work together to shape your reactions, emotions, and relationship patterns. First, I give you a simple overview of the nervous system and talk about what it looks like when the nervous system becomes activated. Then, I cover what happens when attachment feels threatened. When a partner's attachment alarm gets activated, people often respond with instinctive patterns like emotional escalation, protest behavior, withdrawal behaviors, or the familiar push-pull dynamic many couples fall into. These patterns are signs of nervous systems trying to regain safety the only way they know how.

Understanding how the nervous system and attachment interact gives you a clearer lens for recognizing your reactions and your partner's reactions. It helps you see these moments not as personal failures but as protective systems and can help you find new ways to return to regulation, connection and, safety.

Looking at the Nervous System

Bear with me. I'm going to be throwing a lot of science at you, but it's easier than it looks, and I'll break it down to make it easy to understand.

The nervous system is often described as your body's command center. Its job is to receive, process, and respond to information. It controls everything from your muscles to feeling emotions. It takes in information, processes it, and triggers reactions. It helps your body respond to the world around you, telling your heart to beat faster when you're scared or to beat slower when you feel safe.

The nervous system (see Figure 3-1) has two parts: the central nervous system (CNS) and the peripheral nervous system (PNS):

- **CNS:** The brain and spinal cord. It processes information, coordinates movement, and supports decision-making. For example, if you touch a hot stove, the CNS receives the information and coordinates a quick movement away from danger.
- **PNS:** All the nerves outside of the CNS. It connects the body to the CNS, allowing communication between the brain, spinal cord, and the rest of the body.

The PNS has two divisions:

- **Somatic nervous system:** Manages voluntary actions like moving your muscles
- **Autonomic nervous system:** Controls automatic body functions like breathing and digestion

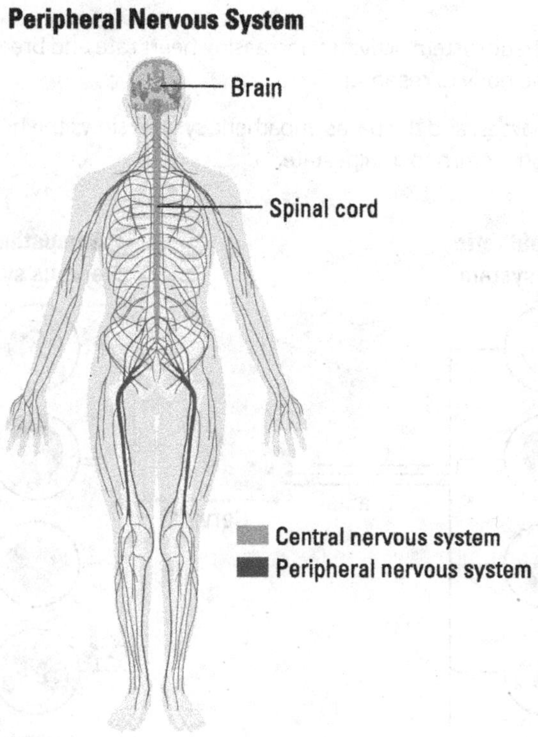

FIGURE 3-1: The nervous system.

The autonomic system is split even further into two systems (see Figure 3-2):

- **Sympathetic nervous system:** Like the gas pedal, kicking your body into action
- **Parasympathetic nervous system:** Like the brake, helping your body to calm down

Your limbic system, which is a group of brain structures, is like a manager that decides which gear your nervous system should shift into based on what's happening around you. Structures in the limbic system include the amygdala, hippocampus, and prefrontal cortex.

The rest of the chapter focused on the ANS, so here's an overview of how it works:

1. A stimulus occurs, such as a sudden loud noise.
2. The CNS quickly processes it.

3. The sympathetic system activates, increasing heart rate and breathing and preparing the body to respond.

4. The threat passes, and the parasympathetic system slows the heart rate and helps the body return to a calm state.

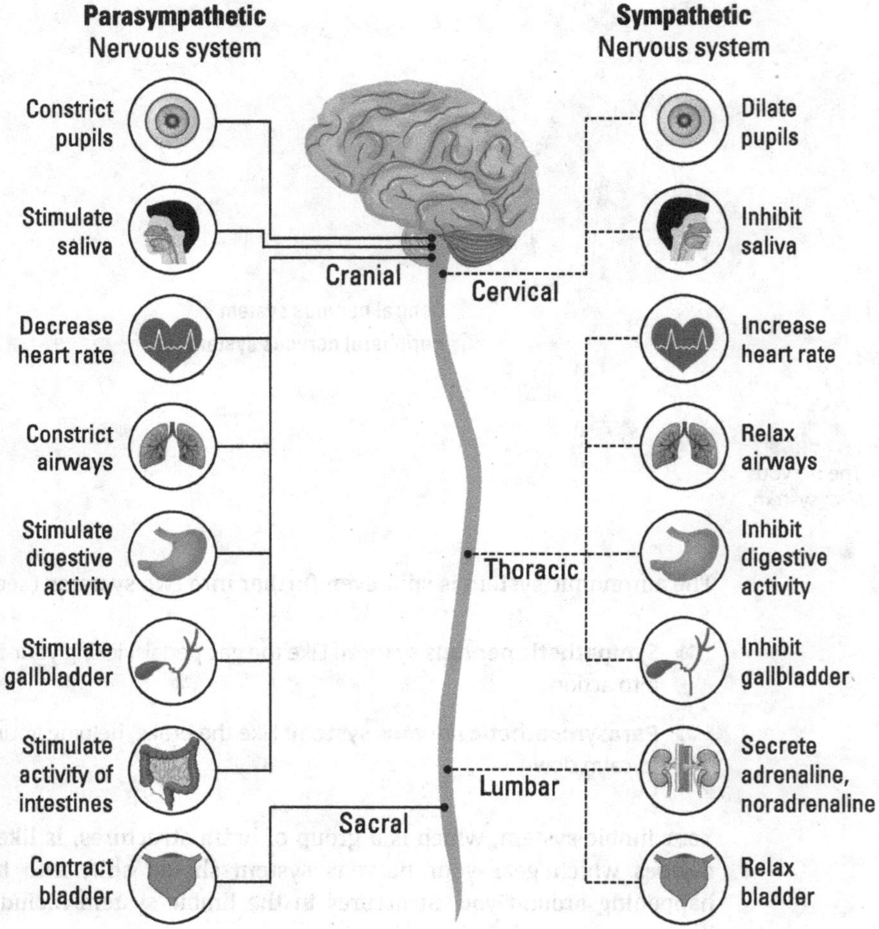

FIGURE 3-2: The divisions of the autonomic nervous system: the sympathetic nervous system and the parasympathetic nervous system.

Exploring the sympathetic nervous system: Activation and protection

The sympathetic branch of the autonomic nervous system mobilizes us for action and protection. Many people refer to the sympathetic nervous system as the fight, flight, or freeze response because it helps the body fight or flee from a perceived or actual threat. Your body automatically prepares to either fight a threat, run away from it, or freeze in place.

When a caregiver is unavailable, threatening, or inconsistent, a child's sympathetic system (SNS) can become chronically activated. Physiologically this looks like increased heart rate, muscle tension, shallow breathing, and a readiness to defend or withdraw. Emotionally, it may manifest as anxiety, hypervigilance, or anger in relationships.

Peeking at the parasympathetic nervous system: Calming and connection

While the sympathetic system puts the body on alert, the PNS supports rest, repair, and connection. It's often referred to as "rest and digest" system. It's what allows the body to return to baseline after stress. It helps you to relax your system.

Through warm, attuned caregiving, a child learns how to coregulate, borrowing the adults calm to soothe their own nervous system. Over time, these repeated moments of repair teach the child that safety and connection are possible even after distress.

Reckoning with an Activated Nervous System

In adulthood, attachment patterns often reflect how our nervous system learned to stay safe. Some people overactivate and pursue connection intensely when threatened (anxious attachment). Others shut down and deactivate to avoid pain or rejection (avoidant attachment). Securely attached individuals can feel activation and self-soothe to move back toward calm connection. Understanding this means seeing emotional reactions as nervous system states, not failings.

Past experiences and attachment injuries all impact whether you become activated and how you react when your systems are activated.

Here are some signs that your nervous system is activated:

- Racing heart
- Feeling hot or shaky
- Tunnel vision

» Urge to shut down, hide, or lash out

» Sudden numbness

EXAMPLE

Marcy hates conflict. The minute she senses tension — a quiet text, a shift in tone — her heart starts to race and her mind spins with stories. She notices herself withdrawing, speaking less, trying not to be seen or "rock the boat." Her nervous system is on high alert, sending signals that danger is near, even though logically she knows she isn't in physical danger. This is her attachment system in action. Because she's experienced that expressing her needs in the past could lead to rejection or anger, her nervous system activates quickly. Her autonomic system kicks in: The sympathetic system gears her up (heart races, shallow breath), while she tries to downregulate by withdrawing or freezing.

Even though Marcy appears quiet and calm on the outside, she's overwhelmed, and her nervous system is flooded with stress signals. If someone presses her for connection or insists on resolving the conflict, her nervous system interprets it as a threat, making it even harder for her to engage or feel safe. Marcy has avoidant attachment, which I discuss more in Chapter 6.

EXAMPLE

Jack feels anxious when he senses even the slightest distance or tension in his relationships. The moment he perceives that his partner might be upset or withdrawing, his body reacts immediately. His chest tightens, and his thoughts race. He wonders, "Are they mad at me? Do they still care?" and he feels a strong urge to reach out, check-in, or fix things. Jack's nervous system is activated. His nervous system interprets potential relational distance as a threat, triggering a sympathetic response: increased heart rate and a sense of urgency. Unlike someone with avoidant attachment who withdraws, Jack's system pushes him toward connection. He seeks reassurance when his nervous system is activated. His mind spins with "what if" scenarios, and he may act impulsively to repair or restore the relationship, even when his partner needs space. Jack has an anxious attachment style. You will read more about this in Chapter 5.

EXAMPLE

Corey loves connection, but it also terrifies him. When he senses conflict, his body reacts in contradictory ways. Sometimes he wants to reach out desperately, and other times he freezes or withdraws entirely. One moment he might text his partner repeatedly, asking if everything is okay; the next moment, he might shut down and avoid responding for hours, leaving his partner confused. When Corey's nervous system is dysregulated, his nervous system sometimes wants closeness, and other times he is fearful and pulls away. This creates a push-pull dynamic. Corey has a disorganized attachment style. You will read more about this in Chapter 7.

EXAMPLE

Even people with mostly secure attachment styles experience nervous system activation sometimes during conflict or disconnection. The difference is in how they respond to the activation.

After a disagreement with her partner, Selene notices a familiar wave of anxiety rising in her body. Her chest feels tight, her thoughts start speeding up, and she feels the urge to immediately seek reassurance. For a moment, she worries that the distance between them could grow into something bigger.

Instead of reacting impulsively, Selene pauses and recognizes that her nervous system is activated. She takes a breath, slows the conversation down, and says, "I'm feeling overwhelmed right now, and I think I'm getting scared that we're disconnecting. Can we take a minute and talk?"

Although the conflict is uncomfortable, Selene is able to hold onto the belief that relationships can experience tension without falling apart. Rather than escalating the conflict or shutting down completely, she works toward regulation, communication, and repair.

Going to Defcon 3: When attachment feels threatened

Defcon 3 is military speak for a high-alert state. This happens when your attachment system feels threatened. In other words, your body thinks something is wrong and prepares to fight, flee, or freeze.

This section is about how partners react to each other when their attachment alarm gets activated in the following ways:

- Emotional escalation
- Protest behaviors
- Criticizing, withdrawing, and shutting down
- Triggering of old attachment wounds

Protest behaviors

Protest behaviors are most associated with an anxious attachment style. They are behaviors that people engage in when they're dysregulated to pull a partner closer. Protest behaviors can show up when you feel:

- Unheard
- Dismissed

- Rejected
- Lonely
- Scared
- Uncertain

The following are some common protest behaviors:

- Pursuing
- Texting frequently
- Saying, "We need to talk"
- Pressuring for reassurance
- Overexplaining
- Expressing fear as anger
- Withdrawing to get attention
- Testing the relationship
- Acting out
- Triangulating

TIP

Triangulating **is when tension or conflict between two people gets pulled into a third person or relationship instead of being addressed directly.**

EXAMPLE

Kirby is in a relationship with Roy. When Roy doesn't answer the phone for hours at a time, Kirby feels worried, insecure, and anxious. Kirby eventually engages in protest behaviors. She does everything from telling Roy she is sick to texting him excessively. If that doesn't work, Kirby then resorts to withdrawing in the hope that ignoring Roy will get Roy to pursue her.

Partners see protest behaviors as controlling, dramatic, reactive, and manipulative. Clinically, the behaviors are expressions of fear, longing, and dysregulation. Chapter 5 covers more about protest behaviors.

Freeze/withdrawal behaviors

Freeze/withdrawal behaviors are most associated with avoidant attachment or disorganized attachment, which are covered in more detail in Chapters 6 and 7, respectively. Here, I provide a brief overview.

Some examples of freeze/withdraw behaviors include:

- Being silent
- Stonewalling
- Changing the topic
- Leaving the room
- Minimizing feelings
- Intellectualizing
- Deflecting blame
- Refusing to engage

EXAMPLE

Sydney is in a relationship with Tyler. When Sydney's attachment becomes activated, he completely shuts down. He cannot tolerate being in the conversation or in Tyler's presence. He leaves, hangs up the phone, and stays gone for many hours.

Push-pull dynamic

When attachment is activated in a push-pull dynamic, you see the following behaviors:

- Seeking intense closeness followed by withdrawal
- Creating emotional distance
- Feeling anger to create space
- Avoiding the partner
- Expressing increased independence
- Showing intense affection
- Engaging in protest behaviors to win back attention

2

Differentiating among Attachment Styles

IN THIS PART . . .

Understand what secure attachment is.

Investigate why some people move closer and crave reassurance when relationships feel shaky.

Uncover why some people instinctively pull away and need space to breathe when relationships feel uncertain.

Explore the nervous-system dynamics of disorganized attachment and how the need for connection can be in conflict with the fear of it.

IN THIS CHAPTER

» Understanding secure attachment

» Anchoring yourself in secure attachment

» Building strong relationships on secure attachment

» Healing with a secure partner

Chapter 4 Exploring Secure Attachment

Secure attachment is not about perfection. It's about having enough safety, enough consistency, and enough responsiveness for connection to feel possible.

For many people who grew up with unpredictability or relational chaos, secure attachment can feel foreign. However, even if a person didn't have secure attachment in childhood, they can learn it, practice it and experience it later in life.

This chapter explores what secure attachment looks like, how it develops, and why it becomes such a powerful resource for healing.

Recognizing the Signs of Secure Attachment

People with secure attachment aren't defined by age, profession, or relationship history, but how they approach connection.

Here are some signs of secure attachment:

- Being comfortable with closeness and independence
- Communicating directly about feelings and needs
- Handling conflict without blowing up or disappearing
- Trusting and willing to let themselves be trusted
- Being able to set boundaries without guilt
- Repairing themselves after rupture
- Seeking support when needed
- Managing disagreements constructively (mostly)
- Often being warm and empathetic and understanding others' emotions
- Having resilience and bounce back after setbacks

EXAMPLE

One person who is securely attached may be recently divorced and navigating dating again, is able to speak openly about what they want, and notices quickly when something doesn't feel right. Another person, after years of relationships that never quite settled, now chooses partners who are emotionally available and isn't afraid to walk away from a relationship when their partner isn't. A third, younger person who's still finding their footing professionally holds steady expectations about commitment and repair inside a long-term relationship.

These three individuals differ in temperament, life stage, and experience. What they share is an underlying expectation that close relationships be responsive, respectful, and safe.

Basking in Secure Attachment

When you're securely attached, you have a sense that your needs matter and you can depend on others. You have a sense that you're allowed to take up space. Connection is safe enough for you to return to it again and again. It's the feeling that you don't have to monitor every moment for signs of danger, and you don't have to protect yourself from being too close with others. Secure attachment is a healthy relationship built on trust, consistency, responsiveness, and emotional safety.

To bask in secure attachment is to rest in the warmth of being known. It means you don't have to stay hypervigilant, perform, or anticipate rejection. You can simply be. In a securely attached relationship, comfort, support, and closeness feel nourishing rather than overwhelming. You can reach for connection without fear, and you can pull back for solitude without feeling like you're risking the relationship. This is what emotional safety feels like.

EXAMPLE

Marisol grew up in an immigrant household where survival came first. Her father remained in Mexico for the first eight years of her life, navigating paperwork and saving money. Her mother worked two jobs in the United States to keep the household afloat. That meant Marisol spent long stretches of time alone. She packed her own lunches, walked herself to school, and figured out most things without guidance. Marisol had two loving parents, but there just wasn't enough time, money, or parental bandwidth for attentive connection or much nurturing. Her parents were stretched thin. By the time Marisol reached her teens, she'd learned the classic avoidant-attachment moves:

- I don't need too much.
- I don't ask for help.
- I don't expect anyone to stay.
- I stay independent and don't burden people.

She was the friend who never cried, the partner who seemed easygoing because she rarely expressed a need. But Marisol also felt a deep, private exhaustion from holding everything together alone.

Things began to shift when she spent two summers with her grandparents in Mexico. Her grandparents were available. They were the first people in her life who had enough time and emotional bandwidth to show care in a steady relaxed way. Her grandfather would sit on the porch with her for hours, listening to her stories. Her grandmother cooked her favorite foods and tucked her hair behind her ear when she was tired. There was no pressure to perform or achieve. This gave her a sense of how safe connection could feel.

Seeing Secure Attachment as Your Life's Anchor

When I think of an anchor, I think of something that keeps a vessel steady. Something that holds the ship and its passengers safe even when the waters shift. Secure attachment functions the same way in relationships. When you're securely attached, you know you can step away and return, explore, and reconnect. You have a secure base. (Read more about having a secure base in Chapter 2.)

A securely attached person can temporarily separate without spiraling into anxiety or fear of abandonment.

Researchers have consistently found that secure attachment in childhood lays the foundation for healthy relationships later in life. Emotional health in adulthood is deeply influenced by the safety and consistency a child experiences with their caregivers because early relational steadiness shapes an internal sense of security.

An internal sense of safety is:

» An inner knowing.

» The bodily sensations and cues that signal you're safe, grounded, and okay.

REMEMBER

This internal anchor can be built through consistent caregiving in childhood, but it can also be developed later. Adults can cultivate this sense of safety through a combination of gentle self-talk, self-soothing strategies, and both cognitive and body-based approaches to healing.

EXAMPLE

Josh grew up in a home where his caregivers were steady and emotionally available. No one was perfect, but the rhythm of his childhood felt predictable. There were morning routines, warm greetings, and adults who noticed him when he was overwhelmed and helped him settle his emotions. Those early experiences taught him that people could be trusted. It also shaped how safety felt and registered inside his body. As an adult, Josh *feels* securely attached. When his phone buzzes with an unexpected message from his boss or his partner, his first response isn't panic.

EXAMPLE

Margaret was raised in a single-parent household. She didn't know her father, and her mother Peggie was unpredictable and emotionally unavailable a lot of the time. Peggie was a functional alcoholic who worked long hours and was out drinking many nights. The result was many lonely nights for Margaret.

Margaret focused on school and sports, which helped her to be resilient. Her initial romantic relationships were with partners who weren't available, creating pain and anxiety for Margaret. Through the years, she worked in therapy on healing her anxious attachment style. She wanted to choose a partner who was available and willing to do work on their self. Margaret started working on her self-talk, her internal working model, and her ability to regulate her emotions. She also had grandparents who modeled secure attachment for her. She knew what it looked like. Eventually Margaret met Mark, whom she formed a secure attachment with.

Recognizing Secure Attachments as the Foundation for Strong Relationships

Research shows that secure attachment is one of the greatest predictors of happiness in relationships. Secure attachment is associated with high levels of relationship satisfaction.

Other findings show that relationships function better when two partners are secure. In couples with mixed attachment styles — with one secure partner — there was an interesting finding: A secure partner helped insecure partners move into a more secure space.

One helpful study for understanding how partners shape each other's attachment comes from a year-long project that followed more than 170 couples across five time points. The researchers wanted to see whether one partner's sense of security in the relationship could influence the other partner over time. The researchers found something surprisingly hopeful: Partners tend to move together in their felt security. When one person's sense of safety and steadiness in the relationship increased, their partner's security usually rose also. And when one partner felt more insecure or unsettled, the other partner often drifted in that direction as well. The authors call this coregulation, which is covered in more detail in Chapter 12.

In practical terms, this means that a securely attached partner can act like an anchor helping an insecure partner feel more grounded, soothed, and steady inside the relationship. This influence doesn't magically transform someone overnight, but it shows that security isn't fixed. It's relational, responsive, and something one partner can influence another in by the way they show up every day.

TIP

Those people who are securely attached have more access to themes such as love, hugs, closeness, and less access to danger. Those who are securely attached are:

- Less defensive
- More flexible
- Willing to express feelings freely
- Straightforward in their desire for closeness
- Forgiving
- Respectful

Healing Life's Wounds with the Help of Secure Partners

REMEMBER

Most people carry around some emotional hurts from the past — moments of feeling unseen, criticized, abandoned, or not enough. A secure partner doesn't erase those wounds. They offer a new emotional environment where those injuries can be tended to. Think of it as slow, repetitive, safe experiences that teach your nervous system that connection can be different this time.

Here are some ways secure partners can be healing:

- **Predictability:** Secure partners are consistent in their words and actions. You can generally anticipate how they'll respond, which builds a sense of safety.
- **Emotional responsiveness:** Secure partners notice your emotions and respond in ways that show understanding and care. They're able to be present with your emotions.
- **Boundaries:** Secure partners maintain healthy boundaries for themselves and respect yours. Boundaries create a safe container for the relationship, so both people can feel free to express needs.
- **Kindness:** Secure partners are secure enough to move toward their partners. They offer empathy and small acts of kindness.
- **Repair after rupture:** Every relationship experiences conflict or misunderstandings. Secure partners acknowledge the rupture, take responsibility when needed and make efforts to reconnect. This sends the message to their partner that disagreements don't have to feel threatening.

EXAMPLE

Maya grew up with a critical mother and learned early to hide her feelings. In past relationships, she went silent during conflict, which usually escalated things. Trevor, her partner, wasn't perfect, but he was steady. When Maya withdrew, he didn't criticize or chase; he simply stayed available. Over time, Maya began voicing small feelings. Trever responded warmly. Maya's nervous system began to rewire. By the time they'd been together two years, Maya's conflict style had changed dramatically. She still felt the urge to retreat, but she was able to say, "I'm overwhelmed. Can we slow down?" Because Trevor consistently met her with calm and clarity, her body learned that connection could be safe.

Recognizing the feeling of a secure attachment

When you're in a relationship with someone who is securely attached, it generally feels pretty stable. Conflict occurs, of course, because conflict is normal. It's normal to have disagreements over things like chores, parenting, money, life goals, and other normal day-to-day things couples bump into. Navigating conflict from time to time is part of any relationship.

What feels different in a securely attached relationship is underlying stability — a steady sense that the relationship is safe even if the conversation is tense. You don't fear that sharing your feelings will blow things up or push your partner away. You don't have to tiptoe or manage their reactions or choose between honesty and connection. You feel safe bringing up your thoughts and feelings.

Generally, in a securely attached relationship you have:

- Stability
- Safety to be yourself
- Open expression
- Consistent reassurance

REMEMBER

Secure attachment allows you to show up fully and relax into the relationship and know your're both seen and safe.

Identifying signs of healing

As you settle into a relationship with a secure partner and begin to feel more secure yourself, you may identify feelings that indicate you're healing, such as these:

- Feeling calmer during conversations that previously felt triggering
- A decrease in anxiety or hypervigilance around your partner
- The ability to pause and respond intentionally instead of immediately reacting
- Feeling confident in expressing your needs without fear of abandonment

Knowing the limitations of what secure partners can heal

REMEMBER

It's important to be clear about what secure attachment can and cannot do. Secure attachment does not eliminate pain, prevent conflict, or erase the impact of earlier life experiences.

Even in the most secure relationships, old attachment wounds can still be activated. Stress, illness, major life transitions, or moments of perceived rejection can awaken earlier patterns of fear, withdrawal, or self-doubt. A secure partner does not magically prevent these reactions from occurring.

What changes is not the absence of these things. It's the way a partner meets these challenges. In secure relationships, distress is more likely to be noticed, named, and responded to with care rather than escalation or abandonment. Over time, this repeated experience helps soften old defenses. Healing is gradual, layered, and nonlinear.

A secure partner can:

- Offer consistency
- Respond with emotional availability
- Set clear, respectful boundaries
- Engage in repair after conflict

REMEMBER

While secure partners can be profoundly healing, they cannot do the internal work on your behalf. They can't replace self-reflection, emotional responsibility, or personal growth. Those are things each person has to do for themselves.

Adapting when secure attachment feels unfamiliar or uncomfortable

Secure attachment is often described as calming, steady, and safe. Yet for many people, especially those who didn't grow up with consistent emotional care, security can initially feel strange, flat, or even unsettling. This reaction doesn't mean something is wrong. It means the nervous system is encountering something new.

TIP

For individuals with anxious attachment, which is covered in more depth in Chapter 5, emotional intensity often becomes linked with connection. High highs and low lows may feel familiar, even reassuring, because they signal engagement and importance. In this context, calm can feel confusing or even boring.

A secure relationship may lack:

- Dramatic reunions
- Urgent reassurance
- Emotional volatility

Instead, it offers steadiness and predictability. For an anxious nervous system, this absence of intensity can be misinterpreted as lack of interest and passion. Thoughts such as *something must be missing* or *if it were right, it would feel stronger* may come up not because the relationship is deficient but because this person is used to operating in a state of activation.

TIP

Over time, as the nervous system learns that closeness does not require constant vigilance, calm begins to feel less like boredom and more like relief.

Being suspicious of consistency

For individuals with avoidant attachment, which I cover in Chapter 6, consistency can feel intrusive rather than reassuring. When a partner is reliably available, emotionally open, and interested in closeness, it may trigger discomfort rather than safety.

Instead of thinking *I am cared for*, an avoidant system may wonder:

- *What do they want from me?*
- *Why are they always here?*
- *When will this become too much?*

Consistency can activate fears of being engulfed, losing autonomy, or being depended on in ways that feel overwhelming.

EXAMPLE

Tessa, who tends toward avoidant attachment, had always valued independence above all else. When her partner Leo, a securely attached partner, consistently checked in, asked about her day, and gently encouraged connection, Tessa found herself feeling uneasy rather than comforted.

Her first thoughts were, *Why is he always checking in? Is he trying to control me? If I pull away, maybe he'll finally leave me alone.* The steady availability that most would interpret as caring instead triggered a subtle alarm: closeness felt like a threat to her autonomy.

Over time, however, Tessa noticed a pattern. Leo's consistency was not conditional or demanding, it was predictable and respectful. Leo never forced closeness and always returned to connection in a gentle, reliable way. Sure, he shared his needs with Tessa, but over time, Tessa came to understand that this was healthy and not invasive. Slowly, Tessa began to differentiate secure consistency from controlling behavior, learning that being close did not mean losing herself.

Misreading secure independence

For someone with an anxious attachment style in particular, availability, responsiveness, and proximity are the cues that the relationship is secure. Because of this, a partner's need for space, alone time, decompression, or independent interests can be interpreted as a warning sign rather than a healthy expression of autonomy.

From an anxious lens, some secure behaviors may be misread as emotional distance, lack of investment or even avoidance. Examples include:

- Taking time to cool off after conflict
- Maintaining friendships and interests outside the relationship
- Not seeking constant reassurance

The anxious system often asks, "If you loved me, wouldn't you need me more?"

EXAMPLE

Lila, who tends toward anxious attachment, had been dating Marcus for six months. Marcus was securely attached and valued both connection and personal time. One evening, after a minor disagreement about weekend plans, Marcus told Lila, "I need a couple of hours to clear my head, and then we can talk." To Lila, this felt alarming. Her first thoughts were, *He's pulling away. Maybe he's losing interest. What did I do wrong?* Her body tensed, and she sent several urgent messages asking if everything was okay. She interpreted Marcus's calm need for space as a lack of investment in the relationship.

Marcus, on the other hand, saw his behavior of taking a short pause to regulate his own emotions before returning to the conversation as normal and healthy. Later, when they reconvened, he was warm, engaged, and fully present. Over time, Lila began to notice that Marcus consistently returned after these pauses, and the brief space was never a threat to his commitment. Slowly, she learned to tolerate and eventually trust his secure independence.

Knowing the difference between secure space and avoidant

REMEMBER

Secure partners do take space, but their space is predictable, clearly communicated, and considerate.

TIP

Secure space usually looks like:

- Saying, "I'll need some time, and I'll come back to this"
- Being emotionally available before and after the space
- Following through on reconnection

Chapters 14 and 16 address more about taking healthy space.

By contrast, avoidant distancing tends to feel:

- Abrupt or unexplained
- Emotionally closed off
- Prolonged or inconsistent
- Disconnected from repair

Anxiously attached individuals may struggle to tell the difference between secure space and avoidant behavior, especially if past partners used withdrawal as a form of punishment or abandonment.

Developing secure attachment involves learning to distinguish space from disconnection.

Over time, repeated experiences of a partner taking space and reliably returning begins to reshape the internal working model, and you can begin to learn the following things:

REMEMBER

- Closeness does not require constant contact.
- Space does not equal rejection.
- Connection can survive pauses.

REMEMBER

This learning happens through practice. Consistency over time is what builds trust.

IN THIS CHAPTER

» Understanding anxious attachment

» Riding the roller coaster of anxious attachment

» Dealing with the complexities of anxious attachment

Chapter 5
Exploring Anxious Attachment

Anxious attachment style is often misunderstood as being clingy, needy, or "too much," but underneath, it's a deep longing to feel secure. People with anxious attachment don't want to overwhelm their partners or their loved ones. They desire to be in stable relationships that feel safe. People with anxious attachment are usually sensitive to changes and uncertainty. They want reassurance that they matter, that they won't be abandoned, and that the relationship is safe enough to relax into.

This chapter explores what anxious attachment really is. In a person with anxious attachment, in early relationships, when connection felt uncertain, their body learned to stay hypervigilant and attuned to signs of distance or disconnection. In adulthood, this can show up as overthinking, checking, protesting, or working too hard to keep a relationship.

Living on the Edge

Anxious attachment is characterized by a longing for closeness and a fear of disconnection. For people with anxious attachment style, relationships can feel scary. They have a need for reassurance from others.

A person with an anxious attachment style will worry even when things are good. There are underlying questions, such as:

- » Is this going to last?
- » What if I lose them?
- » What if I do something wrong?

This happens because the nervous systems of anxiously attached people learned that connection could change easily. They learned to pay close attention, scan the environment for changes, and to stay on guard. Small clues such as change in tone, a certain facial expression, or an unanswered text triggers feelings of fear and anxiety.

Here are some signs of the anxious attachment style:

- » Preoccupation with relationship closeness
- » Heightened worry
- » Overthinking and rumination
- » Emotional reactivity
- » Clinginess and reassurance seeking

Riding the Wave: Managing the Ups and Downs

People with anxious attachment style often live in a cycle that has highs and lows because their attachment system is sensitive. When connection feels strong, they feel calm, present, and hopeful. When connection feels uncertain, they become filled with worry and self-doubt; in some relationships, they may even feel panic.

This section focuses on understanding that cycle.

Noticing the symptoms of the anxious attachment style

Here, I've broken symptoms into emotional, cognitive (thoughts), and behavioral symptoms of anxious attachment:

- Emotional symptoms
  - Feeling easily rejected or hurt by small changes in tone or behavior
  - Fear of abandonment or being replaced
  - Difficulty calming down after conflict or disconnection
  - Persistent worry about the relationship or partners' feelings
  - Mood swings tied to perceived closeness or distance
  - Feeling "too much," "needy," or ashamed after reaching out
- Cognitive symptoms
  - Overthinking text messages, comments, or facial expressions
  - Assuming the worst when something feels off
  - Ruminating about what you said or did
  - Interpreting neutral cues as negative
  - Making up stories in your mind to make sense of uncertainty
  - Difficulty trusting that the relationship is secure
- Behavioral symptoms
  - Clinginess
  - Need for reassurance
  - Jealousy
  - Overanalyzing
  - Poor boundaries
- Physiological symptoms
  - Increased heart rate
  - Anxiety
  - Decreased appetite
  - Feeling constantly on edge
  - Impulsivity/outbursts

Having the language: Let's talk about protesting

If you have read up on anxious attachment or you watch attachment related content on social media, you've probably heard of protesting. Protesting is one of the hallmark behaviors of anxious attachment and has become a well-known term in relation to romantic relationships and anxious attachment.

Protesting is someone's attempt to get attention when they feel unsafe, uncertain, or abandoned. Some clinicians use the term *attachment seeking behavior* or *activated attachment responses*, but they all mean the same thing. These behaviors are adult expressions of the same separation protest that John Bowlby saw when infants were separated from their caregivers. The babies would cry or cling to their caregivers. (Read more about John Bowlby's description of protest behavior in infants and children during separation from their caregiver in Chapter 1.)

When anxious attachment is activated in adulthood, protest behaviors look like:

- Clinging, hyperfixation, and reassurance seeking
- Texting, provoking jealousy, threatening to break up

EXAMPLE

Monique grew up in a family where both of her caregivers struggled with substance misuse, which made them unavailable to her and her siblings. Monique was raised by her aunt who loved her. Despite that, Monique had a strong abandonment wound, and her anxious attachment style often showed up in her relationships. Throughout her relationship history, when her partners wanted space, Monique engaged in strong protest behaviors. She would not give them space. When she recently had an argument with her partner, she texted excessively for days and even threatened to harm herself. Monique was engaging in protest behaviors in an attempt to soothe her attachment system. Her protest behaviors were saying, "I'm scared; pay attention to me."

WARNING

It's important to have awareness of protest behaviors because they can often backfire. Although people engage in them to get closer to their partners, the behaviors often cause the opposite reaction.

REMEMBER

When researcher John Bowlby talked about protest behaviors in infants (see Chapter 1), he described these behaviors as unconscious. This is the reason it is so important for adults to have awareness of their feelings. When you have awareness, you can bring unconscious thoughts and feelings into conscious behaviors, and you can choose different ways to seek closeness.

Seeing how anxious attachments play out in relationships

Once you start to recognize what anxious attachment looks like, you can begin to spot it pretty quickly. However, without an understanding of attachment, you may misinterpret the behaviors that go along with anxious attachment. A partner may come across as clingy, anxious, or demanding, and your first instinct might be to feel defensive, irritated, or frustrated. If you tend toward avoidant attachment, you might even start to pull away from your partner.

When you're able to view these behaviors through an attachment lens, you can begin to think about what might be happening for your partner at the time they demonstrate these behaviors. You can begin to use curiosity and empathy rather than escalating or withdrawing.

EXAMPLE

Carly and Matt have been dating for two years, and they live together. They spend a lot of time together and enjoy making memories together. They travel together, attend family events together, and talk about building a life together. Although Carly grew up in a home that was mostly safe, she had a sibling who developed an addiction, which caused fear and uncertainty in Carly's upbringing.

One of the thing Carly loves about Matt is his calm demeanor. The relationship mostly feels consistent and predictable which is healing for Carly's nervous system. Carly and Matt came into therapy to better understand what happens when they have conflict. During conflict, they end up in the same cycle repeatedly. In a recent therapy session, Carly discussed how she feels when Matt comes home from work. She reported that Matt doesn't greet her. Instead, he sits on his phone in his office. When this happens, Carly gets a tense feeling in her chest and stomach. She worries that something is wrong. She feels uncertain and uncomfortable, and she reacts to that by texting Matt, "Are we okay? Did I do something to upset you?" Her anxiety shows up by increased contact. She asks if everything is okay and tries to make plans for them to reconnect. Carly wants reassurance. As Matt begins to feel overwhelmed, he pulls back further with shorter replies. Carly has an anxious attachment style.

EXAMPLE

Jack and Christopher have been together for five years. They come to therapy because Christopher feels constantly rejected while Jack perception is "nothing I ever do is enough."

Jack grew up in a family where there was a lot of chaos. Due to his upbringing, Jack's nervous system needs a lot of decompression time. This is triggering for Christopher. A typical trigger is when Jack comes home and is less emotionally available after work. Christopher notices that Jack is quieter and less engaged, and Christopher's attachment alarm becomes activated. His chest gets tight; he has racing thoughts and a sense of urgency. Christopher starts to think *I'm not important. Something is wrong between us.* Christopher attempts to be more connected with Jack by asking repeated questions and seeking reassurance.

If Jack reassures him, Christopher feels calm temporarily. When reassurance fades, his anxiety returns. Christopher's attachment profile looks like this:

- Christopher grew up with inconsistent emotional availability from caregivers.
- Christopher became attuned to changes in tone, timing, and responsiveness.
- Christopher has a core fear: *If I'm not actively connected, I'm at risk of being left.*
- Christopher engages in protest behaviors: repeatedly texting when Jack is quiet, asking for reassurance, and bringing up relationship issues.

The key is to disrupt the system and understand what an activated nervous system looks like in anxious attachment:

» Without an attachment lens, Christopher may be labeled as needy and insecure.

» Through an attachment lens, Jack can understand the behavior is understood as

- A nervous system attempting to prevent loss
- A learned survival strategy from earlier relational inconsistency

EXAMPLE

Brandy notices her partner is quieter than usual one evening. There has been no conflict, yet, Brandy's body responds as if something is wrong. She lashes out at her partner, becomes defensive and sarcastic. What is happening in Brandy's nervous system?

Once Brandy perceives possible disconnection

- Her sympathetic nervous system activates
- Her body prioritizes restoring proximity
- Her cognitive flexibility narrows — in other words, her thinking becomes more rigid

Common experiences include:

- Tight chest
- Urgency to act
- Racing thoughts
- Heightened vigilance to tone, timing, and facial expression

As Brandy's nervous system activation increases, her ability to regulate decreases. She becomes less curious and more emotionally reactive. Her system sends a signal: *Connection is threatened, you must DO something now.*

People see from the outside, such as her partner, see the following behavior:

- Brandy asks for repeated reassurance.
- She escalates emotionally when answers feel insufficient.
- She pursues closeness urgently.
- She feels unable to pause or sit with her feelings.

REMEMBER

Anxious attachment disrupts the system by causing a person to:

» Mistake emotional distance for danger

» Prioritize "closeness now" over regulation

Until the nervous system settles, the individual cannot access:

» Perspective

» Secure communication

» Emotional flexibility

Table 5-1 lists some of the possible responses a person with anxious attachment may experience in response to a trigger or threat.

TABLE 5-1 Trigger or Threat Responses

Type	Response
Emotional	Intense feelings
Cognitive	Ruminating, catastrophizing, hypervigilance, interpreting neutral as negative
Behavior	Reassurance seeking, clinginess, people pleasing, impulsive actions
Feedback loop	Negative perception or conflict reinforces anxiety creating cycle of hyperactivation

It's Complicated: Complexities and Triggers of Anxious Attachment

In the examples of anxious attachment in the preceding section, the people were in a mostly safe and responsive relationship and their anxious attachment wound is activated by shifts in closeness and distance. However, it's important to note that there are other situations in which an anxious attachment becomes activated in response to ongoing threats to connection. Sometimes a person becomes anxious not because of their attachment history but because the relationship that they're in is in a period of genuine instability.

Across different situations — substance misuse, emotional unavailability, or an affair — the nervous system is responding to real relational instability. Alongside the heightened alertness and hypervigilance, there is almost always grief. Grief for the relationship that was believed to exist and for a sense of safety that has been lost for a future that was imagined. Often this grief is compounded by a sense of rejection. In these contexts, anxiety is a natural and understandable response to betrayal, loss, and relational uncertainty.

In this section, I give some examples and talk about the anxiety that results from the stress created by these situations.

Substance misuse or addiction

When a partner is struggling with substance misuse or addiction, relationships suffer deeply. The relationship begins to feel unpredictable and even emotionally unsafe. There may be long stretches of instability, chaos, and uncertainty. Trust may erode as honesty decreases. Emotional absence also becomes more common as loved ones get deeper into their addiction. There are also very real concerns about safety and health.

Loved ones may find themselves flooded with questions:

- Is my partner okay?
- Will they stop using or drinking?
- How bad is the problem?
- Do they need treatment?

This constant uncertainty requires the nervous system to remain hypervigilant or "on guard."

EXAMPLE

Laney and Brandon dated for three years before they got married. They had strong chemistry, a solid friendship, and all of the things that made for a secure attachment. Laney was in law school while they were dating, and Brandon worked as an electrician. When she was available, they went to football games and enjoyed socializing. When Laney was working or studying, Brandon hung out with his old buddies. He started drinking and took pills from time to time. Before he knew it, he had a pill habit. Over time, Brandon's addiction took over his life and his relationship. Laney lived in a state of worry over whether he was using or sober or whether he was honest or dishonest. Her nervous system was constantly activated. She searched his phone and home to look for signs of his substance use. Laney developed an anxious attachment style.

Emotional unavailability

When a partner is emotionally unavailable, the relationship may feel distant, one-sided, or chronically lacking in responsiveness. Although the partner is physically present, they may lack emotional attunement. When someone is emotionally attuned to you, it means that they have a sense of how you're feeling and what's happening with you. When emotional attunement is missing, a partner may seem distracted, dismissive, or emotionally flat. Overtime, this lack of responsiveness creates uncertainty within the attachment system. This is a natural response to repeatedly reaching for connection and not receiving it.

An affair

Both emotional and physical affairs deeply impact the attachment bond. In my practice, I've worked with thousands of couples navigating infidelity repair. I consistently see the same pattern: Attachment safety is deeply ruptured, and one partner often begins to experience a cascade of intense emotional and physiological responses. These responses closely resemble what is often seen in families affected by addiction: uncertainty, dishonesty, and a persistently activated nervous system. Trust becomes fragile, hypervigilance increases, and the betrayed partner often finds themselves scanning for danger, checking phones, or accounts, and searching for answers or reassurance.

EXAMPLE

Barbara and David were married for 25 years and had two sons together. David worked for a marketing company, and Barbara was a teacher. Barbara and David had become so busy with their careers and children that they stopped communicating or focusing on their marriage. They still loved each other; they just had stopped nurturing the relationship in the way they once did. They entered therapy when Barbara discovered that David had an affair. Barbara was devastated and highly anxious. She was constantly flooded with questions:

- How could he do this?
- How long did this go on?
- Did he have feelings for this person?

- Did he think of me?
- Were there more affairs?
- What else did he lie to me about?

Her nervous system was in overdrive. She had trouble sleeping, spent time going over all of her previous text messages to David, as well as going through his phone. She threatened to leave David. She even pretended to talk to another man. She was on edge when David left the house, and she needed reassurance throughout the day. Barbara was in anxious attachment.

When anxious attachment shows up under stress

While anxious attachment patterns are often studied in individuals who consistently display them, even individuals with a history of secure attachment may temporarily display anxious patterns under stress. In addition, people who have worked through their anxious attachment style may find the anxiety is reactivated due to life triggers such as a significant loss or grief.

For example, consider a situation in which an individual's child experiences rejection within their social or school environment. Even someone who currently has a secure attachment style may suddenly experience anxious attachment tendencies. In such cases, the individual may feel a profound longing for connection and reassurance from their broader community and experience heightened worry about belonging or being supported.

This scenario highlights the sensitive nature of anxious attachment. Research indicates that situational stressors such as rejection or perceived social threat can temporarily activate anxious attachment behaviors in adults, demonstrating that secure attachment does not make someone immune to attachment-related vulnerabilities (Mikulincer & Shaver 2007; Fraley, 2002). The interplay between emotional activation, rumination, worry, and behavioral responses shows the complexity of attachment.

Understanding these dynamics emphasizes the importance of self-awareness and intentional regulation. When you can recognize what conditions help your anxious attachment parts to emerge, it helps you to be less reactive even under stress. Read more in Chapter 12.

IN THIS CHAPTER

» **Avoiding emotional intensity and maintaining distance**

» **Looking at avoidant patterns and the costs of this attachment style**

» **Understanding why avoidant types couple with anxious types**

» **Keeping an avoidant nervous system present**

Chapter 6
Exploring Avoidant Attachment

Have you ever been in a relationship with someone who keeps a certain distance from you? Someone who tends to keep you at arm's length even when they clearly care about you? Or maybe you've caught yourself pulling away when relationships start to feel too close or demanding.

Avoidant attachment is one of the main ways people handle closeness and emotional connection. People with this style tend to value independence and self-reliance, sometimes to the point where they avoid intimacy, suppress feelings, or keep their distance from others, even when they have deep feelings for them.

This chapter explores what avoidant attachment looks like and why it develops.

Living on the Island: The Pain of Emotional Distance

Imagine standing on a small island surrounded by water. You can see other people on the shore waving and calling to you, but something keeps you from swimming across. That's what life can feel like for someone with avoidant attachment. Living on this emotional island doesn't mean someone is cold or uncaring. It just means that they struggle with letting others in.

Here are some signs of possible avoidant attachment:

- Someone pulls back when things get emotionally intense.
- A person may prefer to do things alone rather than asking for help or sharing feelings.
- They sometimes minimize their own needs or brush off problems instead of talking about them.
- Close relationships can feel uncomfortable or overwhelming, so the person creates a little distance to feel safe.

EXAMPLE

Alex and Jordan are in a relationship. Jordan values connection. When something feels off, Jordan wants to talk it though, understand what's happening, and feel reassured that the relationship is solid. When Jordan reaches out emotionally, it's an attempt to feel close and secure.

Alex experiences that same moment very differently. When Jordan asks, "Can we talk about what's been going on?" Alex feels a tightness inside. It's not that Alex doesn't care, it's that the conversation feels exposing, overwhelming, and risky.

So Alex does what feels safest. She changes the subject. She says she's tired. She reassures Jordan briefly but keeps things at surface level.

Understanding why distance feels safer than connection

For someone with an avoidant attachment style, distance feels like protection. Getting close to others usually means sharing feelings, asking for support, and relying on someone else. All of these things can feel risky to someone who's ever felt hurt, rejected, or overwhelmed by closeness in the past. When connection once came with disappointment or pressure, the nervous system learns that staying removed is safer.

Emotional distance helps those with an avoidant attachment style to feel more in control. By keeping their inner world private, they decrease the chances of feeling exposed or dependent. They don't have to worry about needing too much, being let down, or feeling trapped by someone else's expectations. From the outside, this can look like independence or self-sufficiency, but on the inside, it's often about managing anxiety and staying emotionally regulated.

Over time, creating distance becomes a reliable coping strategy. It helps them avoid feeling vulnerable, keeps uncomfortable emotions at bay, and provides a sense of safety. The challenge is that while distance protects them from pain, it also deeply impacts intimacy and connection. This can be a pretty lonely place to be.

REMEMBER

Keeping emotional distance is about self-protection. Distance helps someone with an avoidant attachment style:

- Avoid feeling vulnerable
- Stay in control
- Manage anxiety

The distance is a coping strategy, a way to protect themselves from pain.

Missing things when you keep your distance

Keeping emotional distance can feel safe, but it often comes with losses that aren't always obvious at first. Many people with an avoidant attachment style don't experience these losses as sharp pain. Instead, they show up as a sense that something is missing, even when life looks fine from the outside.

When you stay emotionally guarded, you miss out on being deeply known by others. Conversations can stay practical or surface level, and while that can feel comfortable, it also limits intimacy. Friends or family members may want to connect more deeply but aren't sure how to reach you, which can leave them feeling shut out or unsure of where they stand.

You may also miss opportunities to receive support from others. Handling everything on your own can feel like strength, but it can also mean carrying stress, sadness, or fear alone. Over time, this can contribute to depression.

Research shows that people with avoidant attachment tendencies are more likely to experience depressive symptoms over time, especially when they rely on emotional distance as their way of coping. Studies find that both avoidance and anxiety in adult attachment are linked with higher reports of depression, lower positive mood, and difficulties with emotional regulation.

The strategies that once helped someone stay safe — minimizing needs, suppressing emotions, and handling stress alone — can increase vulnerability to feeling disconnected, unsupported, and emotionally worn down over time.

REMEMBER

Emotional distance doesn't eliminate the need for connection. The need is still there, and the distance just makes it harder to connect. Some things that are often missed include:

- Feeling truly known and understood by others
- Receiving support during hard moments
- Achieving emotional closeness that deepens trust
- Feeling relief of not having to do everything alone

Peeking behind the Emotional Wall: How Avoidant Patterns Show Up in Relationships

Those with avoidant attachment styles often surround themselves with an emotional wall that keeps others at a distance. This avoidant pattern is not about being uncaring; it's about safety and habit. For someone who grew up needing to protect themselves, emotional self-reliance has become the default mode. In relationships, this pattern can feel like a wall, making someone hard to reach and slow to respond, and sometimes it's frustrating for partners who long for deeper connection.

EXAMPLE

Joseph and Michelle have dated for three years. Joseph is calm, capable, and independent. He went into the military at a young age. He came to the United States from Honduras when he was ten years old, and he lived in a multigenerational household in with his cousins, aunts, and uncles. Joseph was struggling with the move from Honduras to the states. Joseph began to cope with the transition and his sadness by distancing himself from his feelings. He developed an avoidant attachment style. On the surface, he's easygoing and reliable, but like many people with an avoidant attachment, he carries an emotional wall that keeps others at distance.

Joseph's partner Michelle came from a loving yet chaotic household. Michelle was mostly secure in relationships; however, her anxious attachment style was often triggered by Joseph's distance. When Michelle came home from work and asked, "How was your day?" Joseph responded with minimal information. This left Michelle wondering what was happening.

When Michelle shares something emotional, Joseph's instinct is to problem-solve. If Michelle says, "I'm overwhelmed at work and feeling unappreciated," Joseph responds with practical suggestions such as "You should talk to your supervisor" or "Maybe it's time to update your résumé," or he doesn't respond at all.

What Joseph doesn't realize is that Michelle isn't always looking for an answer. She's wants to feel heard, understood, and connected in the moment. When that doesn't happen, Michelle feels alone with her feelings, even though Joseph is physically present and trying to help.

Another layer of this dynamic is Joseph's delayed emotional processing. He often doesn't know how he feels in real time. Emotions tend to register hours, days, or even weeks later, if they register at all. When Michelle asks questions in the moment, Joseph genuinely doesn't have much to say. He's not being avoidant on purpose; his nervous system learned long ago to keep moving forward rather than slow down and feel.

REMEMBER

It's important to note that avoidant attachment isn't always a result of childhood neglect or abandonment or being overwhelmed. People develop avoidant strategies for many reasons including:

- Personal temperament or natural sensitivity to emotional intensity
- Family or cultural norms around independence and emotional expression
- Past relationship experiences that reward self-reliance
- Individual preference for autonomy and self-protection

Understanding deactivation

When intimacy or emotional exposure activates distress, avoidant attachment relies on a process called *deactivation*. Deactivation is a way of regulating closeness by turning attachment needs down and restoring emotional control.

People with an avoidant attachment style avoid emotional exposure. Over time, they develop reliable tools that help them stay regulated, functional, and independent. These strategies are learned adaptations that once served an important purpose.

One common tool is problem-solving instead of engaging emotionally. When feelings come up, the avoidant partner shifts into action mode by offering solutions, making plans, or minimizing the issue. That approach feels productive and safe, whereas sitting with emotion can feel inefficient, overwhelming, or unnecessary.

Another tool is delayed emotional processing. Many avoidant individuals don't have immediate access to their inner emotional experience. Feelings register later — sometimes days or weeks after an event — and may surface only once distance and safety are restored. When asked how they feel in the moment, they may genuinely not know.

Avoidant partners also manage intimacy by keeping communication factual and contained. They share information, logistics, and outcomes but often leave out emotional context. This allows them to stay connected without feeling exposed or vulnerable. To a partner who values emotional sharing, this can feel like distance or omission, even when no secrecy is intended.

These tools help avoidant individuals remain steady and self-reliant. The cost is that emotional intimacy requires skills they may never have learned, such as identifying feelings, tolerating vulnerability, and trusting that closeness won't lead to overwhelm or loss of control.

Avoidant deactivation often feels like calm, clarity, or competence rather than emotional shutdown. The feeling someone with avoidant attachment feels after withdrawing is often relief.

Understanding what avoidant partners often fear

People with avoidant attachment styles often have fears that are quiet, unspoken, and outside of conscious awareness. They may not state these things to their partners, but if you can recognize what avoidant attachment looks like, it can give you some understanding of someone is behaving a particular way.

One common fear is being overwhelmed. Emotional conversations can feel unpredictable and consuming. People with avoidant attachment styles often a worry that once feelings are opened, they won't be containable and the conversation will spiral, escalate, or never end.

Another fear relates to losing autonomy. For avoidant partners, independence isn't just a preference; it's a form of safety. Emotional closeness can feel like a demand or obligation, even when no demand is being made. The fear isn't of the partner; it's of losing control over one's inner world.

Many avoidant individuals also fear doing emotions "wrong." Without a clear roadmap for identifying or expressing feelings, vulnerability can feel risky. There may be a concern about saying the wrong thing, being misunderstood, or being pulled into emotional territory they don't know how to navigate.

Finally, people with an avoidant attachment style often fear burdening others. Avoidant partners may believe that their emotions are their responsibility alone. Sharing feelings can feel selfish, unnecessary, or unfair, especially if they learned early on to manage things on their own.

REMEMBER

These fears don't mean that avoidant partners don't care. In fact, they often reflect a deep sense of responsibility, self-containment, and protection of themselves and of the people they love.

Paying the Cost of Staying Distant

People often push down, ignore, or put feelings aside, especially difficult ones like sadness, anger, fear, or shame. A person usually does this unconsciously to stay composed, avoid conflict, or maintain control.

However, suppressing emotions doesn't make them disappear. Instead, it changes how a person experiences and respond to their feelings, often a cost. In this section, I explain what cost staying distant can have.

Increasing internal stress

Suppression usually means inhibiting the outward expression of an emotion or trying not to think about it while still feeling it internally. Research finds that suppressing emotional expression doesn't reduce the experience of the emotion. It may even *increase* physiological stress, despite the lack of visible expression of the emotion.

When you hold emotions in, your body still reacts. Studies show that suppressing emotional expression is linked to increased sympathetic nervous system activation, the same system that drives fight or flight responses. (Read more about attachment and the nervous system in Chapter 3.)

One way the nervous system can be affected is that when people try not to feel or think about something, those thoughts and feelings tend to come back stronger and more persistently, especially under stress. In other words, suppression can amplify stress rather than reduce it. It's the opposite reaction of what a person is going for.

REMEMBER: DON'T THINK ABOUT THE WHITE BEAR

The phrase *white bear problem* comes from a famous challenge by Russian writer Fyodor Dostoevsky. He dared people to try *not* to think about a white bear. The problem? The harder people tried not to think about it, the more the image popped into their minds.

Psychologists later studied this idea and found something important: When you try to force thoughts away, your brain often holds onto them even tighter.

This shows up in attachment. An anxiously attached person may tell themselves *Stop worrying that they're pulling away*, only to become even more preoccupied with the relationship. An avoidantly attached person may try to suppress their need for closeness, only to become more aware of their discomfort and vulnerability.

The takeaway: Pushing thoughts away usually doesn't make them disappear. Often, it helps more to notice the thought, name it, and let it pass instead of fighting it.

Psychologists call this the *ironic process*, and it's sometimes referred to as the white bear problem. When you actively try not to think about something, your brain has to keep checking whether the thought is still there. One part of the mind tries to distract you, while another part scans for the very thing you're trying to avoid. Under stress or fatigue, that monitoring system takes over, and the thought comes back louder and more persistently. This is why suppressed thoughts and feelings tend to resurface at night, during conflict, or when your guard is down, showing up as intrusive thoughts or emotional flooding. (Read more about emotional flooding in the "Watching for avoidant attachment in conflict" section later in this chapter.)

EXAMPLE

It's like telling yourself *Whatever you do, don't think about a pink elephant.*

Your brain immediately must picture the elephant to check whether you're thinking about it. The same thing happens with emotions.

When someone thinks *I don't want to think about this thing. I'm fine. I'm not upset*, their nervous system keeps returning to the very feeling they're trying to escape.

Cognitive and memory costs

Sustained suppression draws on cognitive resources. Over time this can result in:

- » Reduced working memory capacity
- » Difficulty recalling emotionally relevant information
- » Mental fatigue and slower emotional processing

Social and relational consequences

When emotions are consistently contained rather than shared, a person can face consequences in their social connections and relationships. Here are some examples:

- » Partners feel shut out or unimportant.
- » Emotional attunement decreases.
- » Misunderstandings increase.
- » Intimacy erodes.

Suppression versus acceptance

Suppression aims to control emotion by pushing emotions away. Acceptance regulates emotion by allowing it to move through. Acceptance allows emotions to exist without immediately controlling, fixing or minimizing.

Watching for avoidant attachment in conflict

Conflict is where avoidant attachment becomes most visible, not because avoidant individuals are more prone to conflict but because conflict activates the attachment system.

When emotional intensity rises, avoidantly attached individuals often experience a rapid internal escalation: heart rate increases, cognitive narrowing occurs, and the nervous system prepares for threat response. This happens even if the topic of the conflict seems minor.

Different theorists call this emotional intensity different things. Psychologist John Gottman refers to it as emotional flooding, whereas other frameworks describe it as heightened emotional arousal, nervous system overwhelm, or activation.

To regulate this activation, an avoidant person uses these strategies:

- Intellectualizing the issue
- Correcting facts
- Using a critiquing tone or logic
- Shifting to problem-solving
- Withdrawing emotionally or physically

Looking for protest beneath the withdrawal

A *protest behavior* is any behavior that emerges when the attachment system is activated and a need for connection, safety, or regulation is unmet. Protest is often associated with behaviors such as pursuing or escalating that occurs with anxious attachment, but that's not the only attachment type that exhibits protest behaviors.

REMEMBER

With avoidant attachment, protest is demonstrated by moving away. Shutdown is not the absence of attachment activation. It's the expression of attachment distress through withdrawal. Avoidant protest includes any behavior that increases distance when attachment needs are activated. Shutdown is common, but it's not the only form of protest behavior, although it often gets most of the attention (read more later in this section).

Avoidant protest behaviors fall into four main categories:

- Withdrawal and shutdown
- Criticism and irritability
- Overfunctioning and control
- Dismissal and minimization

All avoidant protest behaviors have some things in common:

- They are triggered by attachment activation.
- They create emotional distance.
- They regulate the nervous system.

Shutdown behavior often gets most of the attention because this form of protest is visible and painful for partners. Its higher visibility makes it more easily noticeable. But many avoidant individuals protest long before they shut down when they criticize, control, or minimize.

WARNING

By the time shutdown happens, the system is already overwhelmed.

EXAMPLE

Evan is often described by his partner Maria as emotionally unavailable. During conflict, Evan eventually gets quiet, avoids eye contact, and disengages completely. Maria experiences this behavior as deeply rejecting and painful. Evan's tendency to shut down is what brought them into therapy. What was less visible, however, is what would happen before the shutdown.

Maria had raised a concern about feeing lonely and wanting more connection. Evan initially responded with logic and correction: "That's not fair. I've been working nonstop. I don't know what else you want from me." His tone changed, and he began to focus on the accuracy of her complaint rather than the emotional content. When Maria continued, Evan minimized, "You're making this a bigger deal than it needs to be."

As the conversation continued, Evan became increasingly controlling, suggesting when Maria should bring things up, how she should phrase them, and why her timing is bad. These behaviors are not neutral; they're protest behaviors. They represent Evan's attempt to reduce overwhelm by managing the interaction.

By the time Evan would finally shuts down, his nervous system was already flooded. His heart rate would be elevated, cognitive flexibility was low, and continued engagement felt impossible.

Why Avoidant Attachment Often Pairs with Anxious Partners

In clinical observation and attachment theory research, avoidant and anxious attachment style frequently show up as a common couple dynamic, even though their needs seem almost opposite. This pattern isn't random: It reflects how early attachment experiences shape expectations about closeness, autonomy, and emotional safety and how those expectations get activated in adult relationships.

Complementary fears activate each other

Anxiously attached individuals tend to seek reassurance and closeness because they fear abandonment; avoidantly attached individuals tend to prioritize independence and minimize closeness because they fear engulfment. When these two styles come together, one partner's desire for connection can unintentionally trigger the other's need for distance, creating a recurring push-pull cycle that feel familiar despite being painful.

Familiarity and expectation reinforce pairing

People are often subconsciously drawn to relational dynamics that feel like home, even if those dynamics were distressing in childhood. An anxious partner may be drawn to the avoidant partner's intermittent warmth followed by distance because it mirrors the treatment they received they learned to expect from an inconsistent caregiver. An avoidant partner may find the anxious partner's emotional intensity familiar because it echoes early experiences when emotional expression was overwhelming.

Intermittent reinforcement maintains the cycle

WARNING

The dynamic can trap both partners: Moments of connection followed by withdrawal become a kind of intermittent reinforcement, like a reward that keeps people engaged even when the pattern is distressing. The anxious partner pursues reassurance; the avoidant partner retreats to protect autonomy, which in turn triggers more pursuit.

Research on relationship patterns

Research supports the idea that anxious/avoidant couples show distinctive stress responses and interaction patterns in conflict situations. For example one study with newlywed couples found that anxious/avoidant pairings exhibited greater physiological reactivity (spikes in the hormone cortisol) and difficulties in responding to each other's distress compared with other pairings.

In other words, research shows that these couples trigger each other's stress responses. The more one person reaches for reassurance, the more the other may shut down or pull away, leaving both partners feeling misunderstood and emotionally exhausted.

Research shows that the combination of attachment anxiety and avoidance tends to be associated with lower relationship satisfaction, trust, and commitment than when secure partners are involved. Anxious partners tend to have more intense emotional needs, whereas avoidant partners tend to withdraw in response to those needs, creating a cycle that can erode both partners' sense of security over time.

EXAMPLE

Katie loves closeness and feels anxious when Chad pulls away. Chad values independence and feels stressed when Katie gets too close emotionally. One evening Katie texts Chad:

> Hey, I really want to talk tonight about us.

Chad, who's had a long day, feels cornered and responds:

> I'm tired. Can we do this later?

Katie interprets this as rejection and texts again:

> You're shutting me out. I just want to feel connected.

Chad starts to withdraw more, avoiding calls and spending extra time on work, which triggers Katie even more. Katie increases the texts and tries to initiate conversation. Chad's nervous system spikes, and finally, he shuts down completely, leaving Katie feeling abandoned with high anxiety.

From the outside, it might look like Chad is distant and Katie is clingy. But what's happening underneath is two nervous systems in conflict. Katie's system is seeking connection to feel safe. Chad's system is protecting himself from emotional overwhelm.

The cycle repeats until both feel frustrated, disconnected, and misunderstood, even though neither partner is trying to hurt the other.

Helping an Avoidant Nervous System Stay Present

For individuals with an avoidant attachment pattern, staying emotionally present is not a matter of willingness. It's a matter of nervous system safety. The instinct to pull away is not a rejection of connection but an attempt to regulate internal overwhelm. Understanding what helps an avoidant nervous system remain engaged allows you to move away from pressure and toward conditions that support presence.

Choice over coercion

REMEMBER

Avoidantly attached individuals are more likely to stay emotionally present when vulnerability is optional rather than demanded. Pressure — even well-intentioned pressure — activates withdrawal. When someone feels they *must* share, respond, or emote to be acceptable, the nervous system moves into defense.

Predictability over intensity

High emotional intensity, especially when it arrives suddenly, can feel destabilizing for avoidant partners. Predictability or knowing what is coming and what is expected helps the nervous system stay regulated.

This includes:

TIP

- Having clear boundaries around timing and duration of emotional conversations
- Knowing that conflict will not escalate into emotional flooding
- Experiencing calm repair rather than explosive confrontation repeatedly
- Providing predictability to allow the avoidant partner to remain present without bracing for emotional overload

Pacing that respects processing time

Avoidantly attached individual often process emotions after an interaction rather than during it.

Here are some things that help:

TIP

- Allowing pauses in conversation
- Respecting request for time to think
- Returning to topics once emotions have settled

IN THIS CHAPTER

» Understanding the struggle of wanting and fearing connection

» Weathering the storm of disorganized attachment

» Recognizing the everyday responses of disorganized attachment

Chapter 7
Exploring Disorganized Attachment

Disorganized attachment is often the most confusing and misunderstood attachment pattern for both those who experience it and the partners who love them. Disorganized attachment is marked by sudden shifts between closeness and distance, intensity and withdrawal, which can leave relationships feeling unstable and unpredictable.

This chapter explores the underlying nervous system dynamics of disorganized attachment, with particular attention to the push-pull pattern that emerges when the need for connection collides with the fear of it.

Wanting and Fearing Connection

Disorganized attachment is often misunderstood as inconsistency or ambivalence. It's a paradox: simultaneous longing for connection *and* fear of it.

For individuals with disorganized attachment, closeness does not simply offer comfort; it also triggers alarm. This internal conflict creates what many partners experience as a push-pull dynamic. A person may pursue intimacy, reassurance, or closeness only to abruptly withdraw, shut down, or act in ways that destabilize the bond.

From an attachment perspective, disorganization develops when the person who is meant to provide safety can also be a threat. In adulthood, this unresolved contradiction often re-emerges in intimate relationships, where closeness activates both desire and danger. Intimacy may feel overwhelming rather than regulating, and a person may experience emotional availability as engulfing, intrusive, or destabilizing. At the same time, distance can feel intolerable, can activate panic, or inspire longing. This creates a pattern that is marked by intensity, unpredictability, and confusion for both partners.

TIP

It's crucial to distinguish this dynamic from simple fear of intimacy or avoidance. In disorganized attachment, the system isn't organized around a single strategy (such as distancing or pursuing). Instead, opposing impulses are activated *simultaneously*, leading to rapid shifts in behavior and relational stance.

EXAMPLE

Consider Claire, who deeply values connection and intimacy. Early in relationships, she feels hopeful and engaged. However, as closeness increases, Claire begins to feel unsteady. Commitment and emotional availability create feelings of both longing and alarm. At times, Claire pulls away, becoming uncertain or critical, even as she misses her partner. When distance grows, her fear of abandonment returns, and she seeks reassurance once more. Neither closeness nor distance feels fully safe, leaving Claire and her partner caught in a painful cycle.

EXAMPLE

Elliot deeply wants closeness with his partner, Juan, but he also fears being hurt or abandoned. When Juan tries to be affectionate, Elliot feels a wave of panic and pulls away, sometimes with sarcasm or sudden coldness. Yet moments later, Elliot regrets pushing Juan away and texts apologies or makes grand gestures to reconnect. Juan feels a sense of whiplash — sometimes cherished and sometimes rejected. Juan's never sure which Elliot will show up on a given day. Elliot's internal conflict of longing for love while also fearing it drives the push-pull dynamic, a hallmark of disorganized attachment.

Being Caught in the Storm: The Unpredictability of Disorganized Attachment

Disorganized attachment can feel like being caught in a sudden, unpredictable storm where the skies shift from calm to turbulent without warning. For someone with this attachment style, closeness can trigger conflicting emotions: a deep longing for connection clashes with an almost instinctive fear of being hurt or rejected. The result is behavior that can seem confusing, inconsistent, and contradictory to other people.

A person with disorganized attachment may crave affection from their partner but may also quickly withdraw after a delayed text response sends them spiraling. The person is both reaching for connection and fleeing from it at the same time.

This unpredictability reflects a deeply ingrained internal conflict about being close to others. Recognizing this internal conflict and the dynamic it creates is the first step toward empathy, understanding, and helping both partners (or parent and child) find steadier ways to connect.

Grasping why the push-pull happens

At the heart of disorganized attachment is a tension between two opposing drives: the desire for closeness and the fear of it. People with this attachment style often grew up in environments where caregivers were unpredictable: sometimes nurturing but frightening or emotionally unavailable at other times. Consequently, as the child grew up, their brain received a confusing message: *I need you, but you might hurt me.*

This internal conflict is the source of the push-pull dynamic in later relationships. When someone with disorganized attachment senses connection, they may feel hope and relief but also fear and anxiety. Because of the fear and anxiety, their instinct may be to withdraw, argue, or act out despite the fact that they also secretly crave reassurance. This simultaneous approach and avoid pattern can feel chaotic not only to partners and friends but also to the person who's experiencing the internal war.

TECHNICAL STUFF

Neuroscience helps explain why this happens. The same experiences that taught the person to fear abandonment as a child can make their stress response hyperactive. Oxytocin, the hormone that encourages bonding, can become intertwined with cortisol, the stress hormone, because the same person is inspiring both a desire for closeness and some level of fear. In other words, intimacy may feel comforting and threatening at the same time.

REMEMBER

Most people with disorganize attachment are rarely consciously deciding to run hot and cold. They aren't deliberately pushing others away. Instead, they're unconsciously responding to patterns wired deep in their early experiences.

Viewing this push-pull reaction as a survival strategy rather than a character flaw opens the door to empathy, self-awareness, and eventually, more stable ways of connecting.

Recognizing common triggers of the push-pull

Even in healthy, loving relationships, people with disorganized attachment can experience sudden waves of fear or withdrawal. Certain situations tend to act as catalysts for the internal push–pull switch to be flipped.

Here I list some of the common triggers:

- **Perceived rejection or criticism:** A delayed text, a sigh, or a gentle critique can feel like abandonment. The person may pull away defensively, even if the intention was harmless.

  EXAMPLE

  Ryan and Jamie have been dating for a couple of years. Jamie grew up in a home that was physically safe but had emotional unpredictability. Jamie's mother could be incredibly nurturing. She cooked meals and read books to Jamie and her siblings. She planned social events and had birthday parties and vacations that were filled with joy. Her mother was also anxious, and when she was anxious she could be shaming, harsh, scary, and critical. Jamie leans toward a disorganized attachment style. Throughout the years, Jamie learned to withdraw to protect herself. While she desires closeness with Ryan and has the capacity for it, she also has a strong fear of intimacy. One evening, Ryan takes a few hours to respond to Jamie's text. Jamie interprets this as disinterest, and she withdraws emotionally, even though Ryan's lack of response was simply because he was busy.

  EXAMPLE

  Greer was in a committed relationship with Frankie. Greer openly expressed feelings of love and connection to Frankie. They had both had affairs in their previous marriages. Greer and Frankie had a strong physical and emotional connection and were taking steps to build a life together. One night, their neighbor Molly was at their home watching a football game. Molly and Frankie were cheering together and engaged in sports talk. Greer was filled with feelings of rejection, and she suddenly packed her bags and left. Greer wanted to feel closer to Frankie in that moment but simultaneously feared vulnerability and the possibility of further rejection.

- **Unexpected emotional intensity:** Moments of deep intimacy, vulnerability, or affection can feel overwhelming to someone with disorganized attachment. The closeness they desire also activates anxiety, leading to abrupt distancing or contradictory behavior.

  EXAMPLE

  Dana and Lawrence had been together for a decade. They had a long history of both good and difficult times. Dana had recently set boundaries with Lawrence around his substance misuse. She asked him to leave their home until he could get help. This led to Lawrence going to treatment and getting sober. Dana and Lawrence had to restart their relationship once he got sober. Lawrence was relearning how to do everything sober: work, love, and navigate everyday life. While Lawrence was in a fragile state, Dana was feeling gratitude for his sobriety. One day, Dana expressed deep gratitude to Lawrence during a romantic moment. Lawrence froze or pulled back, unsure of how to respond to such vulnerability. While Lawrence had the desire for closeness with Dana, he also feared the vulnerability that came with opening himself up again. Feeling pulled between his desire for intimacy and his fear of being hurt, he froze and withdrew.

EXAMPLE

Shelly and Mario have been dating for six months. Mario suggests a weekend getaway. Shelly feels excitement, imagining the fun they could have. Then anxiety rises: *What if I say the wrong thing? What if this ruins the mood?* By the time Shelly responds to the invitation, her answer is hesitant, leaving Mario unsure whether Shelly's enthusiastic or reluctant.

» **Conflict or tension:** Arguments can escalate quickly because the person wants resolution while also fearing confrontation. This can result in a mixture of clinging, blaming, or shutting down.

EXAMPLE

Myra and Jake are arguing about household responsibilities. Jake is frustrated with the dishes and laundry, and he expresses his frustration. Myra initially responds by crying. She moves toward Jake and reaches for him. She asks him if he still loves her. Jake tells Myra to calm down. Myra experiences this as rejection. She takes a step back, becomes sarcastic, and withdraws.

» **Stress or life changes:** Transitions such as moving, job changes, or family pressures can amplify the push-pull, making the person more reactive and unpredictable.

EXAMPLE

Blake is smart, capable and committed to his partner Mary. Blake has a disorganized attachment style. He truly wants love and connection, but when things get stressful, his brain starts to view closeness as a trap. Blake's boss sends an email, and Blake's system goes into fight or flight. By the time he gets home, he's completely flooded emotionally. He's fearful but doesn't know how to express this or how to ask for help. Because vulnerability feels terrifyingly unsafe to Blake, when he sees Mary, his desire for closeness comes as an attack. Mary greets him by telling him about their daughter's cold. Blake lashes out, expressing to Mary that she doesn't understand the day he has had. He then goes to the sofa, shuts down, and scrolls on his phone all evening, skipping dinner with his family.

» **Past memories or reminders:** Certain phrases, tones of voice, or situations can unconsciously trigger childhood patterns, even when the current context is safe.

EXAMPLE

Vance and Kristen have a happy, supportive marriage. Vance has a disorganized attachment style. In childhood, Vance's mother regularly used a sharp, high-pitch tone right before becoming overly critical. One evening, Kristen is looking for her keys and says out loud, "Where are my keys?" Because she is frustrated, her pitch changes. Vance's brain immediately interprets Kristen's frustration as an attack. He stops talking, avoids eye contact, and emotionally withdraws.

EXAMPLE

Rhonda is sitting on her couch when her phone buzzes. It's a text from her friend Ellie. The text says, "Can we talk later?". Objectively, Ellie might want to talk about a minor scheduling detail or something that happened at her place of work or even an exciting event that she wants to share with Rhonda. But for Rhonda, whose attachment history has trained her to expect abandonment, the message is triggering. Rhonda's stomach tightens, and she debates whether to respond. Hours later, she finally replies.

REMEMBER

Recognizing these triggers is a critical step for both the person with disorganized attachment and those close to them. Awareness doesn't *prevent* the reactions entirely, but it allows people within the relationships to respond with empathy rather than frustration. Over time, this understanding can create a steadier, more secure rhythm of connection.

Managing the Internal Experience and Everyday Patterns

Disorganized attachment isn't only about dramatic moments; it shows up in subtle, everyday interactions. Thoughts, emotions, and bodily sensations often swirl together, creating a push-pull struggle that feels confusing from the inside and outside.

This internal conflict doesn't appear only in major relationship decisions. For people with disorganized attachment, it often show up in small moments where desires and fears are both activated. The following examples illustrate how the push-pull dynamic can emerge in everyday situations:

EXAMPLE

- **Receiving praise:** Summer completes a project at work. She wants to feel proud but immediately doubts herself: *Do they really mean it? Am I doing something wrong?* She laughs off the compliment, leaving coworkers puzzled.
- **Making plans:** Sammy's partner suggests a date night. Excitement and dread rise simultaneously as he thinks, *I want to go, but what if it goes wrong?* His hesitation communicates mixed signals, even if he intends no harm.

» **Asking for help:** Alissa feels torn. She wants support for a task but fears being judged or burdening someone. She delays asking, vacillating between seeking connection and withdrawing.

Here is a synopsis of how the push-pull dynamic may show up throughout the different phases of a lifetime:

» **Childhood:** Finley freezes when a parent shows frustration or clings inconsistently, afraid comfort might bring hurt.

» **Adolescence:** Jace swings between confiding in friends and retreating when it seems likely that they will judge her.

» **Adulthood:** Sally desires romantic closeness but pulls away when intimacy feels risky.

REMEMBER

Through all stages, the internal tension remains the same: a desire to approach and a simultaneous urge to avoid connection. Understanding this internal experience helps you see that disorganized attachment is not a series of "bad choices" but a persistent pattern rooted in survival instincts.

Listening to the Body Speak

Attachment responses often appear in the body before the mind fully registers them. A person may feel tightness in the chest, fluttering in the stomach, shallow breathing, or a racing heart, which all signal that the nervous system is on high alert.

EXAMPLE

» Jarvis feels his chest tighten when his partner expresses vulnerability, signaling a protective response.

» Lana experiences a fluttering stomach and an urge to run when a friend raises a concern, even if the situation is relatively safe.

Noticing bodily responses is an early form of awareness. While awareness alone doesn't solve the underlying attachment pattern, it gives a person a way to track triggers and understand why they react the way they do, laying the groundwork for the regulation strategies I cover in Part 4.

3 Attachment Theory in Real Life

IN THIS PART . . .

Notice when attachment patterns show up in your everyday life.

Connect the dots between attachment theory and relationships with parents, friends, partners, and even yourself.

Understand what happens when different attachment styles collide.

IN THIS CHAPTER

» Understanding attachment with parents

» Identifying how attachment shows up in friendships

» Uncovering how attachment patterns show up in romantic relationships

» Thinking about attachment in the workplace

Chapter 8
Recognizing Where Attachment Shows Up

Attachment shows up in the moments when a person feels unsettled, overlooked, too much, or suddenly distant. It emerges in the way a person reaches for others, protects themselves, and makes sense of closeness and separation.

This chapter is not about assigning a label to yourself. It's about identifying how to notice where your nervous system acquired its rules for connection and understanding how those rules shape your relationships today.

Attachment patterns first formed in your earliest relationships, but they didn't stay there. They've traveled with you into friendships, romantic partnerships, work, and even your inner dialogue. What once helped you stay safe, connected, or emotionally intact may have been limiting intimacy, creating confusion, or fueling conflict in more recent years — especially if those old strategies no longer fit your current life. Recognizing how attachment shows up with your parents, friends, and romantic partners, and even in work or social groups, helps you separate who you are from how you learned to connect. That awareness creates space — and in that space, new choices become possible.

TIP

As you read this chapter, you may recognize yourself in one relationship but not another. That's normal. Attachment is contextual. For example, many people are more secure in friendships than in romance or more guarded with parents than with partners. The goal is simply awareness and curiosity.

Reflecting on Attachment with Parents

Your goal for reflecting on attachment with parents isn't to evaluate whether your childhood was "good" or "bad" but to gain understanding about how these experiences impacted you and now influence your current relationships. Attachment is shaped less by isolated events and more by repeated emotional experiences. What matters more than what happened once are the things that were consistent, unpredictable, encouraged, and avoided.

REMEMBER

Most parents love their children. Many parents do the best they can with the resources, stressors, and emotional tools they have available at the time.

A child's attachment forms around some core questions:

- Who comes when I'm distressed?
- What happens when I need comfort?
- Did I feel more soothed by closeness or by being left alone?
- Were my parents emotionally predictable?
- Were emotions welcome, or were certain feelings shut down?

Attachment is also shaped by loss, including separations, illness, emotional unavailability, or changes in caregiving.

Recognizing that attachment can be generational

Parents bring their attachment histories into the relationship with their children, often without realizing it. The way your parents responded to your emotions was likely shaped by how their own emotions were responded during infancy and childhood. Comfort, distance, predictability, or emotional restraint are often passed down not as conscious choices but as familiar ways of relating.

EXAMPLE

Luke remembers his father as emotionally distant but reliable. What David later learns is that his father grew up in a household where emotional expression was discouraged, and self-reliance was praised. Luke's father didn't withhold closeness to be cold. He offered what he knew and what felt comfortable to him. Today, Luke notices the same pattern emerging in his own relationships, even though he wants something different.

EXAMPLE

Naomi grew up with a mother who became anxious whenever Naomi was upset. If Naomi cried, her mother immediately tried to fix the problem, reassure her, or make the feelings go away. As an adult, Naomi developed an anxious attachment style and often worries about being rejected or abandoned in relationships.

Years later, when Naomi becomes a parent herself, she notices that her child's sadness or frustration makes her feel uncomfortable and worried. Without realizing it, she rushes to solve problems, offer reassurance, or distract her child from difficult emotions. Although her intentions are loving, her child may learn that big feelings are something to avoid rather than tolerate and work through.

This is one way attachment patterns can be passed from one generation to the next, not because parents intend to create insecurity but because they often parent from the attachment experiences they learned growing up.

Examining your current relationship with your parents

Attachment doesn't end in childhood. For many adults, parents remain emotionally powerful figures. Your current relationship with your parents can offer important clues about your attachment patterns.

You might notice the following things:

- Do you feel emotionally honest with your parents now, or do you edit yourself?
- Are boundaries present, and are they respected?
- Do you feel responsible for your parents?
- Do you slip into a caretaker role?
- Does distance bring relief, sadness, or both?

Untangling the complexity of adult parent/child relationships

Relationships with parents are rarely simple. Many adult children hold multiple truths at once: love and frustration, gratitude and grief, closeness and distance. Attachment patterns don't capture the whole relationship, but they can help explain why certain interactions feel charged, draining, or emotionally confusing, even in families where there was care and commitment.

It's also common for attachment patterns to show up unevenly. A parent may be dependable in some ways and unavailable in others, or they may be emotionally present sometimes and shut down under stress. These mixed experiences often create the most confusion.

EXAMPLE

Rachel describes her mother as loving and practical. When Rachel needed help, her mother made meals, gave rides, and handled logistics. But when Rachel became emotional, sad, angry, or overwhelmed, her mother grew quiet or changed the subject. Over time, Rachel learned to manage her feelings on her own. As an adult, she feels close to her mother in many ways, yet notices a familiar tightening in her body when a conversation turns to emotions.

EXAMPLE

Tom talks to his mother often and describes their relationship as close. His mother worries about Tom, checks in frequently, and wants to be involved in most decisions. When Tom pulls back, his mom feels hurt or anxious. Tom finds himself reassuring his mother or minimizing his own struggles to avoid causing distress. He values their bond yet often feels responsible for managing his mom's emotions.

In relationships like these, emotional closeness can feel either unavailable or overwhelming.

Sometimes the patterns that developed in your relationship with your parents continue to influence how you relate to others. If you experienced inconsistency, loss, criticism, or emotional unpredictability, you may have learned to protect yourself by staying hypervigilant, taking care of others, avoiding vulnerability, or closing yourself off emotionally. These responses often continue to shape your friendships, romantic relationships, and sense of self.

Recognizing these patterns is not about blaming your parents or dwelling on the past. Instead, it can help you understand why certain situations feel so emotionally charged and give you freedom to respond differently. Awareness creates opportunities to build healthier boundaries, develop more secure relationships, and practice new ways of connecting with other.

Recognizing Attachment in Friendships

Attachment in friendships is often overlooked, yet many people experience some of their most painful relational wounds within friendships. Feelings of exclusion, being left out of a group, friendship breakups, shifts in closeness, one-sided relationships, and changes that occur during major life transitions can activate attachment needs and fears. In current times, these issues are often reflected in social media posts that bring up feelings of exclusion between friend groups.

Understanding attachment can help explain why one person may seek more connection and reassurance, whereas another may need space or independence. Close friendships often become important sources of comfort, support, belonging, and emotional safety. They can serve as a secure base during life transitions, losses, celebrations, uncertainty, illness, grief, and other significant life events.

REMEMBER

A secure base is a relationship that provides safety, support, and encouragement while allowing you to grow and explore. Knowing someone is there for you creates a sense of security that makes it easier to navigate life's challenges. Close friends can serve as secure bases during different seasons of life.

EXAMPLE

Mei and Lillian met while their children were both attending kindergarten. They began taking walks after school drop-off three times a week. Lillian was going through a divorce and experiencing grief and loss. Mei was facing some challenges in her own life with her career and relationship. Their friendship became an anchor — a safe spot to land and a safe place to process their life experiences as well as their pain.

EXAMPLE

Celeste, Stephanie, and Whitney lived together in college. They maintained connections through the years and their friendship became an anchor for them. Stephanie lost her mother in her thirties, Celeste went through the challenges of her brother's mental health crisis, and Whitney dealt with family estrangements that brought sadness and grief.

Relationships with friends often activate the same underlying questions:

- Is it safe to need others?
- Can I be vulnerable with this person?
- Will this person be available to me?
- Can I tolerate distance in my friendships?
- What triggers anxiety or avoidance?
- Will I be welcomed or ignored?

- What happens if I express disappointment or ask for more?
- Will I be overwhelmed by closeness?
- Will my friends respect my space?
- Can we have conflict and repair?
- Can I tolerate discomfort, and can my friends tolerate discomfort?

Compared with family relationships and romantic relationships, friendships can develop more gradually and involve more choice about how much time, energy, and emotional investment people share. As a result, attachment patterns may be less obvious at first. Attachment patterns may show up as patterns of approach, avoidance, people pleasing, or quiet withdrawal.

Looking at examples of friendship patterns

Just as attachment styles show up in romantic relationships, they also influence friendships. The same patterns that shape how people approach closeness, trust, communication, conflict, and emotional connection with romantic partners can appear in friendships.

For example, someone with more anxious attachment tendencies may be especially sensitive to signs of exclusion, worry when friends seem distant, or place a high value on responsiveness and reassurance. Someone with more avoidant tendencies may be less comfortable sharing emotions, prefer greater independence, or need more space within friendships. While no single behavior automatically reflects an attachment style, these patterns can provide clues about how people experience connection and belonging with friends.

The following examples illustrate some of the ways attachment patterns may show up in friendships. While no single behavior automatically indicates a particular attachment style, these patterns can offer clues about how people approach closeness, conflict, belonging, and emotional connection. Many of these examples reflect tendencies commonly associated with anxious, avoidant, or disorganized attachment, although people do not always fit neatly into one category and may show characteristics of more than one attachment style.

- **Managing closeness:** Some people keep friendships light, rarely sharing deep emotions. Others invest heavily and feel hurt if their closeness isn't reciprocated.
- **Conflict and repair:** Some people avoid tension, become defensive, or let relationships drift. Others replay interactions, overapologize, or rush to repair.

» **Belonging and loyalty:** Some people feel easily replaceable or fear exclusion. Others overfunction, trying to earn their place in the group.

» **Expectations:** Some people may expect friends to always be available and responsive. When they aren't, it triggers worry or disappointment.

The flip side is a person who may expect friends to keep emotions out of friendships. When friends reach out emotionally, the person may be triggered to be uncomfortable or withdraw.

REMEMBER

These are learned strategies for staying safe and connected.

When attachment wounds flare up

Life stress, grief, or major transitions can amplify friendship attachment wounds. Someone who is usually secure or mildly anxious may suddenly feel clingy, hyper-sensitive, or easily hurt, creating a clash if a friend has an avoidant style or needs space.

EXAMPLE

Jenna is grieving the loss of a loved one. She reaches out repeatedly to her friend Kai for reassurance and closeness. Kai, who tends to need space under stress, pulls back, leaving Jenna feeling rejected and anxious. Both feel frustrated, and the interaction mirrors patterns they learned in earlier relationships.

EXAMPLE

Heidi's son is going through a major life transition. As Heidi navigates this with her son, she feels a strong need for more connection in her son's school community. She latches onto her close friend Nedra. Heidi typically is secure, but under these circumstances she needs more support and connection.

TIP

These examples illustrate an important point: Attachment patterns are often most noticeable during times of stress, loss, uncertainty, or major life transitions. When attachment needs become activated, people may seek reassurance, withdraw, become more sensitive to rejection, or feel a stronger need for connection. Simply recognizing these reactions can help you respond more intentionally rather than automatically.

In my experience as a clinician, most people don't look beneath the surface of behavior. A friend pulling away may be viewed as rejection, whereas a friend seeking reassurance may be seen as needy or demanding. When people develop a language for attachment and begin to understand the needs, fears, and protective strategies that often lie underneath behavior, they can respond with greater understanding and less reactivity. They may recognize that one friend becomes especially sensitive during times of stress, while another needs more space and independence. This awareness does not eliminate conflict, but it can create more empathy, flexibility, and security within friendships.

The tools discussed throughout this book, such as recognizing triggers, regulating emotions, communicating needs, and practicing secure behaviors, can help you respond to these situations in healthier and more effective ways.

Friendship ruptures and loss

As I discuss in the preceding section, friendships can be a source of comfort, belonging, and support, but they can also be a source of pain. Like family and romantic relationships, friendships experience misunderstandings, hurt feelings, unmet expectations, and periods of distance. Sometimes these challenges are repaired. Other times, they lead to significant ruptures or the end of a friendship altogether.

Because friendships are often viewed as less significant than family or romantic relationships, the grief associated with friendship loss is frequently overlooked. Yet friendship ruptures can activate many of the same attachment fears, including worries about rejection, abandonment, belonging, and self-worth.

People often respond to friendship ruptures in different ways. Some may seek reassurance, repeatedly reach out, or become preoccupied with repairing the relationship. Others may withdraw, avoid difficult conversations, or convince themselves they no longer care. These reactions are often influenced by attachment needs and protective strategies rather than the particular friendship.

TECHNICAL STUFF

Friendship losses can be particularly difficult because of something that psychologists call disenfranchised grief. *Disenfranchised grief* refers to a loss that is not fully recognized, acknowledged, or supported by others. While people generally understand the grief associated with the death of a loved one, divorce, or the end of a romantic relationship, friendship losses often receive far less validation and it becomes hard people to talk about or receive support.

EXAMPLE

Kasey and Amelie became close friends in their twenties. They attended the same college, worked together, and spent much of their free time together. Over time, they became an important source of support for one another. They often turned to each other for comfort and reassurance.

The friendship changed when Amelie entered a serious romantic relationship. As she devoted most of her time to her partner, Kasey felt hurt and increasingly disconnected. She began reaching out more frequently, expressing frustration. She didn't have the words to express her hurt and instead lashed out and engaged in protest behaviors.

Amelie felt overwhelmed by the increased demands and gradually pulled away. Neither friend understood that attachment needs and fears were being activated beneath the surface. What appeared to be arguments about time were also fears about closeness, abandonment, independence, and belonging. Over time, the rupture deepened and the friendship ended, leaving both women grieving the loss of a relationship that had once served as an important source of connection and support.

While not every friendship rupture is caused by attachment dynamics, understanding attachment can help people make sense of what happened. In some cases, recognizing attachment needs may create opportunities for repair. Even when a friendship cannot be repaired, understanding the role attachment played can help people grieve the loss, learn from the experience, and move forward with greater self-awareness.

Ghosting, exclusion, and chosen family

Friendship ruptures don't always occur through direct conflict. Some people experience being ghosted by a friend, excluded from a group, or slowly distanced without explanation. These experiences can be especially painful because they often leave unanswered questions and little opportunity for closure.

For some individuals, close friendships serve as chosen family. This may be particularly true for people who have experienced family estrangement, loss, rejection, or limited family support. When friendships function as chosen family, attachment bonds are often especially meaningful. As a result, friendship losses, exclusions, or cutoffs may feel every bit as significant as difficulties within family or romantic relationships.

TIP

Although friendship ruptures can be painful, they can also offer valuable opportunities for growth and self-understanding. Some people find healing through journaling, writing an unsent letter, seeking support from trusted friends or a therapist, and reflecting on the attachment patterns that may have contributed to the rupture. Even when a friendship cannot be repaired, understanding the role attachment played can help people make sense of the loss and move forward with greater clarity and compassion for themselves.

Dealing with Attachment in Romantic Relationships

Romantic relationships combine emotional closeness, physical intimacy, and high stakes. Your nervous system notices immediately when needs are being met (or aren't).

Here are some ways attachment shows up in romantic relationships:

- **Seeking closeness or space:** You may crave constant contact or pull away under stress.
- **Conflict reactions:** Arguments may feel catastrophic, or you may avoid conflict entirely.
- **Emotional signaling:** You may feel anxiety, defensiveness, or jealousy, or you may overapologizing.
- **Repeating patterns:** You may gravitate toward partners who unconsciously activate familiar attachment dynamics.

EXAMPLE

Collin becomes clingy when his girlfriend is busy, reflecting early patterns of needing reassurance from caregivers.

EXAMPLE

Jaqueline shuts down emotionally whenever her partner expresses frustration, mirroring how she handled her father's criticism growing up.

Recognizing these patterns helps you pause before reacting automatically. Instead of assuming your partner's behavior is entirely about the present moment, you can begin to consider how attachment affects fears, expectations, and protective strategies.

Navigating Attachment in Work and Social Settings

Even work relationships, teams, and social groups can activate attachment patterns. Here are some ways attachment may show up in the workplace:

- **With authority figures:** You may seek approval, avoid conflict, or feel threatened by criticism.
- **With peers:** You may overcontribute to gain acceptance or withdraw to protect yourself.
- **Feedback and recognition:** Praise may feel deeply satisfying or hard to believe, depending on your early attachment experiences.

EXAMPLE

Colby always volunteers for extra work to gain recognition from his boss. Later, he realizes that he tends toward an anxious attachment style and is repeating childhood patterns of seeking validation from caregivers. The awareness of this pattern help Colby in his future interactions at work. As he develops an awareness of this tendency, he's able to work on soothing his anxiety instead of overworking.

EXAMPLE

Bobby tends to lean toward a more avoidant attachment style. He prefers to handle problems on his own and rarely asks coworkers for help, even when he feels overwhelmed. When supervisors offer support or ask how Bobby is doing, often he responds with "I'm fine" and quickly changes the subject. Although he values his colleagues, he keeps personal concerns private and avoids depending on others. Over time, Bobby realizes that his strong self-reliance developed early in life when he learned that expressing needs or vulnerability did not consistently lead to comfort or support.

EXAMPLE

Tara shows some characteristics commonly associated with disorganized attachment. She wants positive relationships with her coworkers and supervisor, but she often feels conflicted about trust. At times, she seeks reassurance and worries about how others perceive her. At other times, she pulls back, becomes guarded, or assumes criticism is coming even when none has been expressed. A brief piece of constructive feedback can leave her feeling anxious, while praise may feel difficult to believe. As she learns more about attachment, Tara begins to recognize a familiar pattern: wanting connection and support while simultaneously fearing disappointment, rejection, or being let down.

REMEMBER

Many adults spend a significant portion of their lives at work. Attachment patterns can influence everyone in the workplace. Managers, supervisors, business owners, and leaders may also experience attachment-related reactions to workplace events such as conflict, criticism, promotions, layoffs, and employee departures. Understanding attachment patterns can lead to improved communication and better emotional regulation in the workplace.

Some professions also expose people to intense emotional experiences that can create particularly strong workplace bonds. Medical professionals, first responders, therapists, military personnel, and others who face high levels of stress, crisis, or emotional intensity together often develop deep connections with colleagues.

Navigating attachment in the workplace can be especially challenging because work relationships require a balance between connection and professionalism. Unlike close personal relationships, employees often depend on supervisors and coworkers for opportunities, feedback, recognition, and job security. As a result, attachment concerns about approval, rejection, trust, or criticism may be activated, even when relationships remain professional. Learning to recognize these reactions can help people respond more thoughtfully rather than automatically repeating old patterns.

IN THIS CHAPTER

» **Understanding your attachment style**

» **Looking at your partner's attachment style**

Chapter 9
Diving Deeper into Attachment

Attachment styles are adaptive strategies people develop to stay connected and safe. Before you can change your patterns in relationships, you have to have awareness of what your attachment style is.

As they come to understand their attachment styles, many people begin to think things like this:

- *Oh . . . this is why I react that way.*
- *This explains why we keep having the same fight.*

EXAMPLE

Amanda and Jonathan entered therapy saying, "We keep having the same fight over and over."

Amanda felt hurt and anxious when Jonathan pulled away during conflict. When he became quiet, she pursued him harder, asking questions, demanding reassurance, and sometimes raising her voice. Jonathan, on the other hand, felt overwhelmed when emotions escalated. When Amanda pushed for closeness in those moments, Jonathan shut down even more and needed space to calm himself. Once they began learning about attachment styles, something shifted. Amanda realized, "When he pulls away, I panic. I assume I'm losing him." Jonathan realized, "When she gets emotional, I feel like I'm failing. I shut down so I don't make it worse."

A REVIEW OF ATTACHMENT STYLES

Earlier chapters go into deeper descriptions of the four attachment styles. The following table is a brief reminder.

Attachment Style	How They Show Up in Relationships	What You May Notice in Yourself or Your Partner
Secure	Comfortable with closeness, communicates openly	Can ask for support and give support easily
Anxious	Seeks frequent reassurance, may worry about partners	May feel clingy, fear abandonment, or overanalyze interactions
Avoidant	Values independence, may pull away in conflict	May keep distance, avoid deep conversations
Disorganized	Mix of anxious and avoidant behaviors	Push-pull patterns, confusion about closeness and safety in relationships

They were reacting from old strategies designed to protect connection and safety. Amanda showed anxious tendencies. Jonathan showed avoidant tendencies. Awareness helped them slow down the cycle instead of repeating it.

In this chapter, I help you uncover your attachment style and help you reflect on what type of attachment style your partner may have.

Uncovering Your Attachment Style

REMEMBER

Attachment is contextual. You may feel secure with one partner and anxious or avoidant with another.

You can use the following quiz as a tool for the following purposes:

- As a starting point for understanding your attachment style and your partner's attachment style
- As a way to give you and your partner a shared language for talking about your relationship
- As a tool for developing compassion and clarity when interacting with others

This quiz is designed to help you begin exploring your attachment patterns in relationships. Its purpose is not to place you in a rigid box or give you a fixed label but to help you notice the ways you tend to connect, protect yourself, seek reassurance, respond to conflict, and experience emotional closeness. Attachment is complex and deeply contextual. You may feel secure in one relationship and anxious or avoidant in another depending on the level of safety, consistency, communication, and emotional responsiveness in the relationship.

My hope is that this quiz gives you language for experiences you may have felt but struggled to describe. For some readers, the results may bring clarity or validation. For others, they may simply spark curiosity and reflection. Either way, the goal is not judgment. The goal is awareness. When you better understand your attachment patterns, you become more equipped to recognize your triggers, communicate your needs, build healthier relationships, and respond to yourself and others with greater understanding and compassion.

You can also use this quiz as a shared tool within your relationships. Many couples find that attachment language helps them better understand recurring conflict patterns, emotional reactions, and differences in the way each partner gives and receives connection. Attachment theory can help create a more compassionate framework for understanding what may be happening underneath your reactions.

Here's how to take the quiz:

1. **Read each statement and rate how true it feels in your romantic relationships.**
2. **Score using this scale:**

   0 = Not at all true

   1 = Slightly true

   2 = Mostly true

   3 = Very true
3. **Write down your score for each question.**
4. **Score your results.**

   Many people see themselves in more than one category. This is normal. Here's how to interpret your score:

   - Your highest subtotal indicates your primary attachment style.
   - Your second-highest subtotal often shows up under stress or conflict.

Section A: Secure

1. I generally feel comfortable depending on my partner and having them depend on me.
2. I can express my needs without fearing abandonment or rejection.
3. When conflict happens, I believe we can work it out.

Secure subtotal: ________

Section B: Anxious

1. I worry that my partner doesn't care as much as I do.
2. I feel uneasy when I don't hear back quickly from my partner.
3. I often need reassurance that the relationship is okay.

Anxious subtotal: ________

Section C: Avoidant

1. I feel uncomfortable when partners want too much closeness.
2. I prefer to handle problems on my own rather than rely on others.
3. When conflict arises, I tend to shut down or pull away.

Avoidant subtotal: ________

Section D: Disorganized

1. I want closeness, but when I get it, I feel overwhelmed or unsafe.
2. I can swing between craving connection and pushing my partner away.
3. Relationships often feel intense, confusing, or unpredictable.

Disorganized subtotal: ________

Here are some questions to help you reflect on your score:

- » How does my attachment style show up during conflict?
- » What am I most afraid would happen if I were fully honest with my needs?
- » How might my partner's attachment style make sense given their history?

Examining Your Partner's Attachment Style

As yourself the questions in this quiz to reflect on your partner's patterns in your relationship. Answer based on what you *observe* most often, not on assumptions you make.

For each statement, choose the option that feels most accurate: rarely, sometimes, often, almost always.

Scoring (simple pattern recognition):

» Responses to statements 1, 3, 6, and 8 are almost always: Secure tendencies

» Responses to statements 1 and 4 are almost always: Anxious tendencies

» Responses to statements 2, 5, and 7 are almost always: Avoidant tendencies

» A mix of anxious and avoidant patterns: Disorganized tendencies

REMEMBER

Use this quiz as a reflection tool, not a label. The goal is to understand patterns and improve communication.

1. When upset, my partner seeks closeness and reassurance.
   - Rarely
   - Sometimes
   - Often
   - Almost always
2. My partner tends to pull away or need space when emotions get intense.
   - Rarely
   - Sometimes
   - Often
   - Almost always
3. My partner is comfortable expressing emotions and talking about feelings.
   - Rarely
   - Sometimes
   - Often
   - Almost always

4. My partner seems anxious about whether I will be there for them.
   - Rarely
   - Sometimes
   - Often
   - Almost always
5. My partner enjoys independence and sometimes prefers to solve problems alone.
   - Rarely
   - Sometimes
   - Often
   - Almost always
6. My partner values consistency and reliability in the relationship.
   - Rarely
   - Sometimes
   - Often
   - Almost always
7. My partner may get frustrated when I need closeness or reassurance.
   - Rarely
   - Sometimes
   - Often
   - Almost always
8. My partner seems confident in the relationship and rarely doubts our bond.
   - Rarely
   - Sometimes
   - Often
   - Almost always

IN THIS CHAPTER

- » Examining attachment pairings
- » Understanding attachment types and triggers
- » Understanding how different attachment styles impact each other

Chapter 10
When Attachment Styles Clash

From the many couples I've worked with over the years, one core truth keeps showing up: Most relationships aren't failing because people don't care. More often, they're struggling because two nervous systems are reacting in completely different ways, and neither partner understands what's happening inside themselves or the other person.

When attachment gets activated, people aren't just having a disagreement. Their bodies are reacting. One partner may move closer for reassurance, while the other pulls away to calm down. Without awareness, these reactions can feel personal, intentional, and even threatening. And when neither partner knows how to regulate those reactions or help the other regulate, the relationship can start to feel stuck.

Examining the Pairings with Recognizable Patterns

Before I get into the details of how some specific attachment pairings often work, I want to address why I focus on the anxious-avoidant, anxious-anxious, and avoidant-avoidant pairings. Of course, these aren't the only possible combinations. People with secure, anxious, avoidant, and disorganized attachment styles can all form relationships with one another, and in real life, many people also show traits from more than one attachment style.

I focus on the three specific pairings because they tend to create the most recognizable and predictable relationship patterns. Understanding these common dynamics can help you recognize what may be happening beneath the surface of conflict and disconnection.

You may also notice that I don't devote separate sections to secure attachment pairings. That's because secure attachment often functions less like a distinct relationship pattern and more like a person's ability to navigate relationship challenges effectively. People with secure attachment still experience conflict, hurt feelings, and misunderstandings, but they're generally better able to communicate, repair, and work through challenges together.

Disorganized attachment is more difficult to categorize because it often includes both anxious and avoidant tendencies. Depending on the situation, a person with disorganized attachment may seek closeness, pull away from it, or move back and forth between the two. As a result, people with disorganized attachment may recognize parts of themselves in several of the relationship patterns discussed throughout this chapter.

The goal of this chapter is not to cover every possible combination of attachment styles. Instead, it's to help you recognize the most common cycles that emerge when attachment fears become activated in relationships.

Clinging and Withdrawing: The Anxious-Avoidant Relationship

The most common attachment pairing I see in my practice is the anxious-avoidant relationship. In fact, many times I can tell within the first few minutes of a couple walking into my office that this is the dynamic they're caught in.

From a clinical perspective, the pattern becomes clear pretty quickly. One partner tends to show up as more emotionally intense. They may talk more, ask more questions, and appear highly aware of their partner's reactions, often even hypervigilant to small shifts in tone, facial expressions, or silence. They're trying to understand what's happening in the relationship and often push for conversation or resolution.

The other partner often presents very differently. They may use fewer words, struggle to express what they're feeling, or shut down more easily when emotions rise. When conflict begins to build, they may become quieter, more withdrawn, or unsure how to respond.

To the anxious partner, this can feel incredibly frustrating. They see their avoidant partner's reaction as passivity, avoidance, or a lack of willingness to engage. The anxious partner may think, *Why won't you talk to me? Why aren't you doing anything to fix this?*

From the avoidant partner's perspective, something very different is happening. The anxious partner's questions, requests for reassurance, or desire to keep talking may not create a sense of connection in the moment when they come up. Instead, they can feel overwhelming, emotionally intense, or difficult to navigate. The avoidant partner may worry that no matter what they say, it won't be enough to calm the situation. As their stress increases, their instinct is often to pull back, become quieter, or create distance in an attempt to regain a sense of calm. They aren't necessarily trying to reject their partner; they're trying to regulate an overloaded nervous system.

Looking at the anxious-avoidant dance

At first, the two people in an anxious-avoidant partnership often feel drawn to each other. The anxious partner tends to be expressive, emotionally open, and eager for connection. The avoidant partner may seem calm, grounded, and independent. At the beginning, this balance can feel exciting.

But when conflict appears, the very traits that once felt attractive start to trigger certain reactions in each other. You can think of it as an anxious-avoidant dance that goes something like this when conflict hits:

One partner reaches because anxious attachment says *Connection will keep me safe.*

One partner retreats because avoidant attachment says *Independence will keep me safe.*

The anxious partner thinks, *If I push harder, we'll be okay.*

The avoidant partner thinks, *If I get space, we'll be okay.*

The anxious partner asks, checks, pursues, escalates.

The avoidant partner shuts down, minimizes, delays, or distances.

The anxious partner feels abandoned.

The avoidant partner feels suffocated or overwhelmed.

REMEMBER

Both partners are trying to regulate fear. They just regulate in opposite directions.

In Chapter 6, I talk about protest in anxious attachment, which shows up when they feel their partner pulling away. It's the anxious partner's attempt to get the relationship back. Some examples of protest behavior are repeatedly texting a partner after an argument, asking for immediate reassurance, threatening to end the relationship, becoming critical, or picking a fight in an attempt to get a response. Remember, a person doesn't do one (or more) of these things because they want to end the relationship. They do them in an attempt to restore connection.

The anxious-avoidant dance looks like the anxious partner protesting and the avoidant partner pulling away.

Protest → Withdrawal → Bigger Protest → Bigger Withdrawal

REMEMBER

Neither partner is trying to hurt the other. Both are reacting from fear.

EXAMPLE

Nina came into the session ready to talk. Within minutes she was explaining how frustrated she felt when Ethan shuts down during arguments. "He just goes quiet," she said. "I'm trying to fix things, and he won't even respond."

Ethan sat next to her, looking down. When I asked him what was happening for him in those moments, he paused before answering.

"I don't know what to say," he finally said. "When she comes at me like that, it feels like anything I say will make it worse."

Nina immediately jumped in. "But you not saying anything makes it worse!" From Nina's perspective, Ethan's silence felt like abandonment. It made her push harder for answers, reassurance, or some sign that he cared enough to engage.

From Ethan's perspective, Nina's intensity felt overwhelming. The more emotional the conversation became, the more pressure he felt and the more he shut down.

Neither of them were trying to hurt the other. Nina was trying to protect the relationship. Ethan was trying to keep things from escalating. Without realizing it, they had fallen into the anxious-avoidant cycle: The more Nina pursued connection, the more Ethan withdrew. And the more Ethan withdrew, the more Nina pursued.

TIP

Once couples begin to recognize this pattern, something important happens. Instead of seeing each other as the enemy, they begin to see the cycle itself as the problem.

Watching for signs you're stuck in the anxious-avoidant trap

The anxious-avoidant pairing is one of the most common relationship patterns therapists see. One partner moves toward connection when things feel uncertain, whereas the other moves away to regain a sense of calm. Neither person is trying to hurt the other. Both are trying to protect themselves, but their instincts can create a cycle that leaves both partners feeling misunderstood.

Here are a few signs this dynamic may be happening in your relationship.

- **One person pushes more and more, and the other partner pulls away.** In anxious-avoidant relationships, the partners often trigger each other without meaning to. When the anxious partner feels distance, they try to close the gap. They ask questions, seek reassurance, or push to talk things through. The avoidant partner experiences that intensity as pressure. Their instinct is to step back, shut down, or take space.
- **Both partners feel like the other person is the problem.** Over time, this cycle can lead each partner to develop a story about the other. The anxious partner may believe the avoidant partner is cold, distant, or unwilling to care about the relationship. The avoidant partner may believe the anxious partner is overly emotional, demanding, or impossible to satisfy.
- **Conflict leaves both people feeling alone.** Ironically, both partners often leave arguments feeling abandoned. The anxious partner feels alone because the avoidant partner emotionally checked out. The avoidant partner feels alone because they felt overwhelmed and misunderstood during the conflict.

TIP

One of the most powerful moments in therapy happens when couples realize, "This isn't just you or me. This is the pattern we fall into together."

When partners begin to see the pursue–withdraw cycle clearly, they can start working as a team to interrupt it instead of blaming each other.

Spinning Simultaneously: When Two Anxious Partners Pair Up

Sometimes both partners have an anxious attachment style. This type of relationship may feel incredibly passionate and emotionally intense. You may hear people in these couples talk about feeling like they are soulmates early in the relationship.

But when conflict appears, both partners may struggle with fear of abandonment. Instead of one partner chasing and the other withdrawing, both partners are trying to pull the relationship closer at the same time.

In this section, I describe what this looks like and signs that two people with anxious attachment are in a relationship.

Looking at the anxious-anxious spiral

In a relationship with two partners with anxious attachment styles, arguments can escalate quickly. Both partners want reassurance. Both partners want to feel chosen. But when both people are scared at the same time, conversations can become emotional whirlwinds. Small misunderstandings often spiral into big arguments about the future of the relationship.

EXAMPLE

Danielle notices Austin seems quieter than usual during dinner. "Are you upset with me?" she asks.

Austin hadn't been thinking about anything serious, but the question suddenly makes him nervous. "No. Why would you think that?" he says.

Danielle hears hesitation in his voice. "You paused. That usually means something's wrong."

Now Austin starts to worry that he actually did do something wrong. "I promise I'm not mad. Are you mad at me?" he asks.

Danielle wasn't mad before, but now *she* feels unsettled. "I'm not mad. I just want to know if something is going on." Within minutes, both partners are scanning the relationship for signs of danger and thinking about questions like the following:

- *What if we're not okay?*
- *What if something is wrong between us?*
- *What if the other person is pulling away?*

REMEMBER

Neither partner is trying to create a problem. They're trying to protect the relationship. But because both people are anxious about losing each other, the conversation quickly becomes emotionally intense. Their conversation goes from talking about dinner to talking about whether they feel loved, appreciated, and secure in the relationship. All of this started simply because one partner seemed a little quiet.

The pattern two partners with anxious attachment often fall into looks like this:

- When two anxious partners are triggered at the same time, their conversations can escalate quickly.
- Both partners want reassurance.
- Both partners want emotional closeness.
- Both partners want to know the relationship is safe.

REMEMBER

The good news is that two anxious partners can build incredibly strong relationships once they learn to slow these moments down. Instead of asking, "Are we okay?" over and over again, they learn to say things like: "I think my anxiety is getting activated right now."

Watching for signs you're in the anxiety loop

When both partners have an anxious attachment style, the relationship can feel incredibly loving but also emotionally exhausting. The problem is that both nervous systems are constantly scanning the relationship for signs of danger.

Here are a few signs that two anxious partners may be caught in the anxiety loop.

- **Small things turn into big relationship conversations.** A simple moment such as a delayed text message, a distracted look, or a tired tone of voice can quickly turn into a deep conversation about the health of the relationship. Instead of letting the moment pass, both partners begin trying to figure out what it means and ask questions like these:
  - *Are you upset?*
  - *Did I do something wrong?*
  - *Do you still feel the same about us?*

  Before long, what started as a small moment turns into a serious conversation about the future of the relationship.
- **Reassurance works — but only for a little while.** When one partner reassures the other, it helps, but the relief doesn't last very long. A partner might say, "Of course I love you," or "We're okay." For a moment, the nervous system settles. But soon the anxious mind starts searching again for signs that something might be wrong. This doesn't mean the reassurance wasn't genuine. It just means anxious attachment tends to seek constant confirmation of safety.

- **Both partners feel responsible for the other person's feelings.** Two anxious partners often become highly attuned to each other's moods. If one partner seems upset, the other immediately feels responsible for fixing it. This can create pressure on both sides.

TIP

Two anxious partners often have a powerful strength that gets overlooked: They deeply value connection. When these couples learn to slow down their anxiety and tolerate a little uncertainty, they can build relationships that are incredibly emotionally supportive. The goal isn't to eliminate the desire for reassurance. The goal is to learn that the relationship can be safe even when everything isn't perfectly settled in the moment.

Moving Away: When Two Avoidant Partners Pair Up

When two avoidant partners come together, the relationship may initially feel calm and low conflict. Neither partner is overly demanding. Both value independence and personal space. Over time, though, the double avoidant attachment can begin to create challenges.

This section looks at what happens when two people with avoidant attachment are in a romantic relationship.

Looking at the distance dance

At first, two partners who both have avoidant attachment styles may think the situation feels refreshing because of the lack of intensity. Later, though, problems can arise when emotional distance slowly becomes the norm. Difficult conversations may be postponed indefinitely. Needs go unspoken, and vulnerable feelings are kept inside. Over time, the relationship can start to feel more like roommates sharing a life rather than partners who are deeply connected to each other.

REMEMBER

Neither person intends to create distance. But because both partners instinctively protect themselves by stepping back emotionally, intimacy may never fully develop.

EXAMPLE

Lauren and Christian have been together for four years. They rarely fight. Friends sometimes comment on how calm their relationship seems. "We just don't do drama," Lauren says. When something bothers Lauren, she usually decides it isn't worth bringing up. She tells herself she'll get over it. When Christian feels stressed, he throws himself into work or hobbies until the feeling passes. Neither of them likes uncomfortable conversations.

One evening, Lauren mentions that her sister asked why they still aren't engaged. Christian shrugs. "I don't think we need to rush things," he says. Lauren nods and changes the subject. The conversation ends there. Later that night, Lauren feels a quiet wave of disappointment. She wonders whether actually sees a future with her. Christian notices that Lauren seems a little distant, but he assumes she just needs space. So he gives it to her. Over the next few weeks, they both feel a subtle tension neither one fully understands. Lauren stops bringing up long-term plans. Christian works a little later than usual. Distance grows between the two of them.

REMEMBER

Neither partner intends to create disconnection. Both are simply doing what they've always done when emotions feel complicated: handling things alone.

In relationships between two avoidant partners, conflict often isn't explosive. Instead, the challenge is emotional distance. From the outside, the relationship may appear peaceful. Inside, both partners may sometimes wonder whether they're truly known by the other person.

TIP

The work for avoidant couples isn't usually about reducing conflict. It's about learning to move toward each other instead of automatically stepping back when emotions arise.

Watching for signs two avoidant partners are drifting apart

When two avoidantly attached people form a relationship, things may look calm on the surface. There may be very little fighting and plenty of personal freedom. But sometimes the absence of conflict can be a sign that important feelings and needs are staying hidden.

Here are a few signs that two avoidant partners may be slowly drifting apart:

- **Important conversations never quite happen.** In avoidant relationships, difficult conversations tend to get postponed. One partner might think about bringing up something important like finances, commitment, or emotional needs, but then that person decide it's not worth the discomfort. The other partner may sense that their loved one is holding something back but avoids asking too many questions. Over time, big topics quietly pile up beneath the surface.
- **Independence slowly turns into emotional distance.** Avoidant partners often value independence, which can be a healthy thing in relationships. But when both partners lean heavily on independence, they may begin living parallel lives instead of a shared one. They handle their own stress. They

process emotions privately. They solve problems alone. Eventually, the relationship can start to feel more like two individuals sharing a household than two partners sharing their inner worlds.

- **Vulnerability feels uncomfortable for both partners.** Avoidantly attached partners often learned early in life that expressing emotional needs wasn't particularly helpful. As adults, this can make vulnerability feel unfamiliar or even risky. When both partners carry this pattern, moments that require emotional openness such as discussing fears, disappointments, or hopes for the future may feel awkward or quickly brushed aside.

TIP

Avoidant partners often assume that bringing up emotional needs will create unnecessary tension. But in reality, gentle vulnerability is often what builds trust and closeness. For avoidant couples, growth usually begins with small steps, such as saying "I've been thinking about something, and I'm not totally sure how to say it, but I want to try."

REMEMBER

Moments like this can slowly teach both partners that emotional closeness doesn't have to mean losing independence.

4 Moving toward Healing

IN THIS PART . . .

Become aware, intentional, and steady even when your attachment system gets activated.

See how emotions show up, tune into your body's signals and name what's happening, and begin working with your feelings.

Build skills to listen to and comes to terms with your inner voice, reparent yourself, and self-soothe.

Begin to notice attachment patterns of the people in your life and figure out how to make your attachment patterns work with theirs.

Build safer connections with others.

Develop skills to communicate with greater clarify and connection by expressing your needs, creating emotional safety, and managing conflict.

IN THIS CHAPTER

» Recognizing an activated nervous system

» Managing with an overloaded system

» Listening to what the body is saying

» Dealing with old patterns

Chapter 11
Noticing the Cycle

One of the things I often say in sessions with couples is, "We're not just talking about you, and we're not just talking about your partner. We're talking about the dynamic between you."

This chapter is about those patterns. It's about what happens when each of you gets activated, when something in your nervous system gets triggered, and how you tend to respond in those moments. Do you move toward your partner, seeking reassurance? Or do you pull back, shut down, or need distance? Understanding this is the key to having a clear picture of your cycle.

Understanding Attachment System Activation

Your attachment system is a built-in part of being human. It's designed to help you stay connected to the people you rely on for safety, support, and emotional closeness.

When something in a relationship feels off — distance, conflict, disconnection, or even a shift in tone — your attachment system can switch on very quickly. This is what we mean by attachment system activation.

Understanding why the system turns on

REMEMBER

Your attachment system activates when your brain senses a possible threat to connection. That threat doesn't have to be dramatic. Your system can turn on for something as simple as:

- Your partner doesn't respond to a text.
- You detect a change in their tone.
- You feel dismissed, criticized, or misunderstood.
- You sense a moment of distance when you were expecting closeness.

When things like these happen, your nervous system reacts automatically. You're no longer thinking only about the situation. The activation of your nervous system means you feel it in your body.

EXAMPLE

Farren is dating Robin. She sends him a simple message: "Hey what time will you be home?"

Robin responds, "Not sure." There's no warmth and no emoji. Something inside Farren shifts. Her mind starts filling in the gaps.

She thinks, *He must not want to hang out. Why was that so short? Did I do something?* Her system is activated.

EXAMPLE

Nette is sitting with Tucker, and she says, "Hey can we talk for a minute?"

Something inside of Tucker immediately tightens. He immediately things, *Why does this have to be a whole conversation? Things were fine, why are we doing this right now? I don't want to turn this into something big.* Tucker's response is to start behaving differently. He pulls back a little. His system has been activated, and he moves toward a little bit of distance.

TIP

You can think of attachment activation like an internal alarm system.

When your brain senses, *Something about this relationship doesn't feel safe right now*, the alarm goes off. From there, you either try to get closer or try to protect yourself by pulling back. Or you may vacillate between moving toward and moving away, which is a push-pull response. (Read more about a push-pull response in Chapter 7.)

Looking at two common responses

Once activated, people tend to move in one of two directions.

Some people move toward connection, which is what is called *hyperactivation*. They do the following things:

- Seek reassurance
- Ask questions
- Try to fix or resolve things quickly
- Feel anxious or preoccupied

Others move away from connection, a response that's called *deactivation*. It can look like:

- Shutting down
- Needing space
- Minimizing feelings
- Avoiding the conversation altogether

REMEMBER

Hyperactivation and deactivation are two different reactions with the same underlying goal: to feel safe again.

Knowing what most people miss

Both reactions toward and away from someone are your nervous system's best attempt to protect you based on what it has learned over time.

WARNING

But those responses can be tricky because the very things you do to feel safer can sometimes create more disconnection. Your reaction may result in the opposite reaction from the other person:

- The more one person pushes, the more the other pulls away.
- The more one withdraws, the more the other pursues.

And a cycle begins.

EXAMPLE

Angela says, "Hey, we haven't been spending much time together lately. I feel like we're drifting." Her tone has a little urgency in it.

Stuart feels an immediate reaction to Angela's words and tone. His body tightens. He feels pressure. So he responds, "I think you're overthinking this. Things are fine." He pulls back slightly.

Stuart's response doesn't calm anything in Angela. In fact, it does the opposite. Now Angela feels even more activated, and she says, "See, this is what I mean. You never want to talk about things. You just shut down." She is anxious and frustrated. Her tone gets more intense.

Now Stuart feels even more overwhelmed, and he withdraws further. He says, "Why does everything have to be a problem? I don't want to do this right now."

At this point Angela is pushing harder, but Stuart is pulling away faster. Both of them feel misunderstood. Angela is in hyperactivation and Stuart is deactivating.

WARNING

If you don't understand activation, it's easy to:

- Blame yourself
- Blame your partner
- Get stuck trying to "win" the argument

However, when you understand activation, you can recognize see what's happening underneath the surface and make changes. When I work with couples, I see them begin to change the cycle when this understanding and recognition occurs.

EXAMPLE

Jody and Doug came to therapy because of communication issues. I observed that Jody and Doug had a deep connection. They laughed often in session, and I could sense their chemistry and desire to be together. It was obvious.

They had been dating for five years, and Jody expected the relationship to be further along by the point they came to see me. She wanted them to move in together and build a family unit with her three boys. Doug said he loved Jody and wanted to be with her, but he also described feeling pressured. When Jody became more intense about moving forward, Doug would sometimes respond harshly, even saying things like, "I don't love you." When that happened, Jody would become even more activated. She would ask questions like:

- Why are you acting like this?
- You didn't feel this way last week. What changed?
- Can we just talk about this?

In response to the questions, Doug would pull back even further. This was their pattern. And it didn't just happen at home. I could see it happening in the couples session. Both of them were getting activated. Jody would get anxious, and Doug would shut down.

Overloading the System: Activation and Flooding

John Bowlby and Mary Ainsworth described the attachment system as something that becomes activated under conditions like threat, separation, or uncertainty. (Turn to Chapter 1 for more on their pioneering work.) There are a few different ways to describe what's happening in these moments. You might hear it called activation, emotional flooding, or fight or flight. These terms don't describe exactly the same thing, they're all pointing to a similar experience: your body shifting out of safety and into protection.

TIP

When you feel this way, use whatever language helps you to recognize it:

- I'm getting activated.
- I feel flooded.
- My body is in fight-or-flight mode.
- I'm feeling triggered.

If nothing interrupts the activation, your system keeps turning the volume up until it crosses a threshold. Activation can build in intensity, and at higher levels of arousal, it can become overwhelming. This is what John Gottman refers to as *flooding* and Sue Johnson describes as *emotional overwhelm*.

When you're flooded, your nervous system becomes so overwhelmed that:

- Your heart rate increases.
- Your thinking narrows.
- Your ability to respond productively drops.

You experience physical changes and your thinking changes.

REMEMBER

EXAMPLE

Sarah notices that Ron has been more distant lately. He's quieter, less engaged, and seems distracted when they're together. Her system picks up on this shift immediately. She starts to feel uneasy. Her chest tightens, and her breathing shifts a little. By the time she brings up what she's noticed, her tone is sharper than she intended as she says, "Why are you being so distant lately? Are you even happy in this relationship?"

From the outside, her words might sound like criticism, but underneath, something else is happening. Sarah begins to question the whole relationship. Her system is activated, and she moves into hyperactivation, while Ron moves into deactivation strategies.

What Sarah's really feeling is can be described like this:

- Are you pulling away from me?
- Am I about to lose you?
- Do I still matter to you?

Ron hears her question, but he doesn't hear the fear underneath it. His system activates too, and he feels accused, pressured, and like he's already doing something wrong. As a result, he responds by pulling back and says, "I don't know what you're talking about. I'm fine." Or he may even say, "Why do you always do this?"

Ron's response makes Sarah feel even more anxious. Then Ron feels even more overwhelmed. Within seconds, both of them have moved from activation into overload.

When the Body Speaks First

When I work with couples in the therapy office, one of my goals is to bring their attention to their bodies. If you pay close attention to your body, you can usually tell that you're activated or that you're moving toward being activated.

Often your body begins to react before your mind starts to formulate thoughts. Your body has usually registered a threat before your mind begins to spin into different thought patterns. Your heart rate increases, your muscles tighten, and your breathing may even change. These responses happen automatically, and you're typically not conscious of it. A delayed text or change in tone can create a strong physical reaction, and your nervous system responds as if something is at risk.

TIP

If you're talking to your partner and you begin to feel frustrated and anxious, or you notice yourself distancing, ask yourself, *What am I feeling in my body?*

You may notice the following symptoms:

- Tightness in your chest
- A queasy stomach
- Your heart racing
- A tight jaw
- A sudden feeling of irritability
- The impulse to shut down or flee

REMEMBER

When I talk about activation or flooding in my office, I remind couples that when they're in this activated state, they can't think clearly because their brain is no longer fully in charge. Their main job is to get themselves grounded.

TECHNICAL STUFF

When your attachment system is activated, your brain responds as if there's danger, and the amygdala (your threat detector) lights up, just like when you're in fight or flight mode. Instead of your system saying, "I'm in danger," as it does when you're in fight or flight, your system says, "My connection is at risk."

Letting Old Patterns Drive Your Responses

When your attachment system is activated, your brain is doing more than responding to what's happening in the present moment; it's also pulling from what's happened before. Past relationships, early family experiences, and unresolved hurts all shape how you interpret what your partner is doing in the present.

TIP

In session, I often ask, "What is this situation bringing up for you?" You can ask yourself this same question.

For example, if you were hurt in a previous relationship, such as by a partner who had an affair or otherwise betrayed you, you can become highly sensitive to signs of disconnection. In a current relationship, if your partner has a shift in tone, seems less available, or isn't spending as much time with you, the situation may not feel neutral to you. Your system reads these things as potential threats. You may think, *Something's wrong. I could get hurt again. This feels familiar.* The result can be hyperactivating responses like seeking reassurance, overanalyzing, or pursuing your partner more intensely. (See the "Looking at two common responses" section earlier in this chapter for a definition of hyperactivation.)

On the other hand, if you grew up feeling overwhelmed — emotionally or relationally — you may carry a deep sensitivity to closeness. When a partner moves toward you with intimacy, your system may not register it as safe. It may feel like too much. In response, you might pull away, need space, or shut down emotionally as a way to regulate that overwhelm.

People who have never experienced safe, consistent intimacy may feel unsettled when real closeness begins to develop. Even if part of you wants connection, another part of you may not recognize it as safe. Consequently, you may create distance, minimize your needs, or disengage just as things start to feel more real.

TIP

When old patterns are impacting your responses, you're not just reacting to your partner; you're also reacting to the past, and that can be part of what makes relationship dynamics feel so confusing. The intensity of your reaction doesn't always match what's happening in the moment because part of that reaction belongs to the past.

EXAMPLE

Tracey was previously married to Philip. During their relationship, Philip drank frequently and had multiple affairs. Each time Tracey discovered the betrayal, she was devastated. Eventually, the marriage ended in divorce.

In the years that followed, Tracey focused on healing and rebuilding her life for herself and her kids. She dated casually, but nothing serious developed until she met Jacob. Jacob was quiet, kind, and steady. He worked remotely for a tech company and lived a relatively low-key life. Tracey found herself drawn to his calm and stability. Being with him felt different, safer, and more grounded than her relationship with Philip.

However, a few months into the relationship, small moments began to stir something in Tracey. One evening, Jacob didn't respond to her text for several hours. When he finally replied, his tone was warm and normal, but by that point, Tracey's body had already reacted. Her chest felt tight. Her mind started racing. Her thoughts were running: *Why hasn't he responded? Who is he with? Is something going on?*

Without her full realization, Tracey's system had linked the situation to her past. In her marriage, periods of disconnection often meant something was wrong, and something painful she hadn't discovered yet was going on. Her brain had learned to associate inconsistency with betrayal. So even though Jacob hadn't done anything untrustworthy, Tracey's attachment system responded as if he had. She began texting more, asking questions, and seeking reassurance. From her perspective, she was trying to feel safe again. But from Jacob's perspective, the intensity didn't quite match what had happened.

This is how old patterns shape present reactions. Tracey isn't reacting only to Jacob. She's also reacting to what her system learned from Philip. And unless she becomes aware of her system's activation, that past experience will continue to influence how she feels and responds in her current relationship.

REMEMBER

Not all old patterns lead to moving toward a partner. For some people, the pattern shows up as pulling away.

EXAMPLE

Marshall grew up in a home where emotions felt overwhelming. When conflict or closeness intensified, things would escalate quickly, and he often felt like he had no space to breathe. As an adult, when his partner tries to connect more deeply, asking how he feels or wanting more time together, Marshall notices a familiar sense of pressure in his body. His system reads the connection as too much. From the outside, it can look like he's not interested, but that's not the case. What's actually happening is that he is trying to regulate a feeling of overwhelm that started long before the relationship.

If you recognize yourself in this pattern, remember that awareness is the first step. The good news is that attachment patterns can change. In Chapter 12, you find out how to identify and manage difficult emotions through techniques such as emotion labeling, body awareness, and regulation. In Chapter 13, you discover strategies for self-soothing and developing a healthier relationship with yourself when attachment fears arise. Chapter 14 focuses on putting these skills into practice in relationships by learning to pause, manage triggers, and respond more intentionally. Finally, Chapters 15 and 16 help you build the safety, communication, and repair skills needed to create more secure connections.

IN THIS CHAPTER

» **Identifying feelings**

» **Exploring primary and secondary emotions**

» **Rating your emotions**

» **Understanding feelings and coregulation**

Chapter 12
Identifying and Managing Feelings

Identifying your feelings is the first real doorway into emotional security and healthy attachment. Before you can regulate, communicate, or connect, you have to know what you're actually feeling.

In this chapter, I slow things down and talk about how emotions show up as primary feelings that are right at the surface to the secondary feelings that are buried a little deeper. You find out how to tune into your body's signals, name what's happening inside, and begin working with your feelings instead of working against them. The first step is identifying what you're feeling.

Naming It to Tame It: Why Labeling Emotions Matter

Many people who show up in my office don't the benefits of knowing what they're feeling. For some, the idea of knowing your feelings is unnecessary, uncomfortable, or even weak. Their beliefs may come from growing up in a family culture where feelings were ignored or dismissed. In that type of emotional environment, vulnerability is looked down up or doesn't feel useful. Some people view emotional awareness as soft; others don't value emotions as information. Some people worry that if they open the door to their emotions, those feelings may take over. But the truth is, avoiding your internal world doesn't make it disappear.

Here are some benefits of knowing your feelings:

- When you don't attend to your emotions, it doesn't mean they aren't there. They're just suppressed. They come out through irritation, anxiety, or outbursts that impact your relationships.
- When you suppress your emotions, you continue to carry them in the body. This causes tension and physical symptoms.
- Naming feelings gives you clarity and understanding and reduces reactivity.
- Knowing what you're feeling helps you to communicate in a way that helps you to meet your needs.
- Emotional awareness helps you to stay grounded and connected.

EXAMPLE

George is feeling hurt and frustrated that he experiences Lindsay as rigid and dismissive. He doesn't feel heard in the relationship and feels that everything is the way Lindsay wants it to be. George has not taken the time to sort through his thoughts or feelings. He just keeps moving. When George comes home, he slams doors and stays on his phone scrolling instead of engaging with Lindsay. This goes on for years until their relationship becomes more and more disconnected and negative sentiment takes over.

EXAMPLE

Gerard notices that he is feeling some emotions after a conversation with Reece. He wants to identify what is going on within himself. He takes some time to remove himself from the living room and checks in with himself. *What's going on with me? What's bothering me? What am I feeling in my body?* He notices tension in his jaw and his chest. He gives himself time to ponder this. He realizes that he's frustrated and feels unheard in his conversations with Reece. He wants to feel heard and considered in the relationship. He wants his voice to matter. He recognizes that being continually dismissed is creating feelings of frustration and sadness. Knowing his feelings gives him an opportunity to communicate this to Reece instead of shutting down and disconnecting.

Untangling Primary and Secondary Emotions

Emotions can be complicated. Sometimes one emotion hides another emotion. Think about it as if you are peeling an onion. Layer by layer, each feeling reveals more about what's really going on under the surface. The outer layers often contain secondary emotions such as anger or defensiveness. As you peel those layers back, you may discover primary emotions underneath, such as hurt, fear, loneliness, disappointment, or sadness.

Understanding the difference between primary and secondary emotions can help you gain a deeper understanding of your internal world. *Primary emotions* are the core emotions that you feel. *Secondary emotions* are the feelings that develop on top of those primary emotions and can sometimes mask what's really going on underneath.

Here are some qualities of primary emotions:

- Primary emotions are usually immediate and instinctual.
- They are usually sensitive and vulnerable.
- They can help guide you.
- They are usually fear, happiness, sadness, surprise, and anger.

Secondary emotions have these qualities:

- They're reactions to your primary emotions.
- If an emotion lingers, it's usually a secondary emotion.
- Secondary emotions are often learned responses.
- Sometimes secondary emotions have to do with how you feel about the primary emotion, as in these examples:
  - Feeling ashamed because you're angry
  - Feeling guilty because you're sad
  - Feeling embarrassed because you're scared
  - Feeling resentful because you're hurt

REMEMBER

Secondary emotions can make the primary emotion harder to recognize.

EXAMPLE

Parker got into a car accident. His immediate feelings are sadness and fear. Later, Parker becomes irritated by the other driver, the construction being done on the street, and his wife.

Parkers primary emotions are sadness and fear. His secondary emotions are irritation and frustration.

Once you know your primary and secondary emotions, you can improve your emotional regulation by responding to the primary emotion rather than reacting impulsively to the secondary emotion. In the preceding example, if Parker is not aware of his primary emotion, he's at risk of snapping at his wife or others because his secondary emotion is irritation.

REMEMBER

When you can pinpoint your feelings, you're in a better position to manage them and to develop coping strategies for them.

TIP

You can ask yourself these questions to separate primary and secondary emotions:

» What was the first feeling that I felt physically and instinctively?

» What story am I telling myself about that feeling?

» Am I judging myself for this feeling?

REMEMBER

Primary = instinctive, raw

Secondary = commentary or reaction

TIP

Practice makes identifying emotions easier. The more you do it, the faster you can identify the feelings and the layers.

Using the feelings wheel as a visual aid

For many, emotions feel abstract until they can see them. Robert Plutchik and Gloria Wilcox are two people who believed that emotions make more sense when a person can visually see them.

In 1980, Robert Plutchik created the wheel of emotions to show how emotions relate to each other. Gloria Wilcox created the feelings wheel in 1982, and it has become a useful tool in therapy offices everywhere. When clients can visually follow the emotion, they find it easier to identify what it is that they're feeling. It's common for someone to go from feeling fine or frustrated to identifying feeling sad, worried, disappointed, and conflicted when they use the feelings wheel to identify what emotion they're feeling.

One of the goals of using the feelings wheel is to move from vague to specific. Being able to name specifically what you feel is one of the foundations of secure connection with yourself and others.

TIP

Place the feelings wheel in an area that is convenient to you or have a couple of copies, such as a magnet on your refrigerator or a copy in your office, car, or purse. The whole family can use feeling wheels. Doing so gives everyone a chance to become more familiar with their feelings.

The feelings wheel has this structure:

- The primary emotions, such as sadness, anger, and happiness, are in the middle.
- As you move outward, the emotions become more specific, such as confused, proud, lonely, or disappointed.

Here are three ways to use the feelings wheel:

- To identify your feelings, start in the center and identify your primary emotion, such as sadness, and then move outward to identify specific words such as lonely or disappointed.
- Make it a routine to do a feelings check once or twice a day.
- Identify your feelings and then journal about them as a way to further understand them and process them.

TIP

You can use the wheel when you're feeling triggered, activated, or emotionally flooded (three different ways to describe feeling full of emotion). When you're in this emotional space, the wheel can be a helpful tool that for identifying your emotions and getrinf clarity.

EXAMPLE

Karen has an avoidant attachment style. When Karen is activated, she pulls away or withdraws. This makes her partner Lucia feel abandoned and hurt. They went to couples therapy to work on healing their attachment styles. Their therapist suggested that they use a feelings wheel to help with regulation. When Karen becomes triggered, she and Lucia have agreed to take a break in the conversation. During the break, they both look at the feelings wheel to identify emotions. This enables them to come back together with clarity and specific words. Karen can return to the conversation and share feeling "tired and scared" instead of shutting down. Lucia can hear Karen and also share her feelings. Together they have learned how to regulate themselves and each other.

Aligning with yourself: Body scan

The body often knows what your mind hasn't realized yet. Tight shoulders, a knot in your stomach, or shallow breathing can tell you what you're feeling.

The body scan, which originated in Buddhist practice, is a widely used tool in psychotherapy for increasing awareness of physical sensations and helping people to connect to their emotions. It's a simple practice in which you do a mental scan from head to toe. You can do it anywhere for any length of time. It only takes about 30 seconds if you are short on time.

A body scan helps you do the following:

- Increase awareness and notice where you carry stress or emotion
- Track physical signals of primary and secondary emotions
- Calm your nervous system and be present

You scan your body and pay close attention to any sensations you notice. Here are steps to do a body scan:

1. **Find your space.**

   You can do a body scan anywhere — your office, your car, or your bedroom. It's up to you to decide where you feel comfortable. You can sit down or lie down.

2. **Start at the top of your head and move through your body parts, spending five to ten seconds in each area.**

   Slowly work your way down your body:

   - Head and face, paying attention to your eyes, cheeks, and jawbone
   - Neck and shoulders
   - Arms and hands
   - Chest and heart area
   - Stomach and gut
   - Back and spine
   - Legs and feet

3. **Notice any sensations.**

4. Ask yourself these questions:

- What do I notice?
- What feeling am I carrying there?
- What color is it?
- How big is it?

EXAMPLE

Sophia was driving to work. She could tell something was off with herself, but she couldn't put her finger on it. She had been feeling needy in her relationship, calling her partner excessively, as well as feeling physical anxiety when he didn't answer the phone. Sophia's anxious attachment style was triggered by grief, but she didn't recognize it yet. She stopped the car in her office parking lot, sat still, and closed her eyes. Her therapist had told her about the body scan, and she decided to try it. She started with the top of her head and passed through her cheeks, her neck, and her jaw. She paid close attention to any sensations. As she got to her chest, she felt tightness. If she could give the sensation a color, it would be orange.

She asked herself, *What is that tension in my chest? It feels like fear. What happened that scared me? What am I afraid of?* She waited for the answers. She suddenly remembered the call she got Thursday about her father's cancer. She started to cry in the parking lot. She put her hand on her chest and soothed it. She felt an immediate release after crying. Once she pinpointed her feelings, she was able to manage them better. It made sense to her that her grief was coming out sideways. She was able to validate her feelings by saying to herself, *Of course you're sad and scared and worried. You received hard news. You're going through a tough time.* She was able to give herself some validation and grace. With this awareness, she was able to communicate to her partner and they worked together to coregulate. (Read more on coregulation later in this chapter in the "Regulating and Coregulating" section.)

EXAMPLE

Patick's mother was an alcoholic. For Patrick and his siblings, this created chaos, fear, and unpredictability. When he was 14 years old, Patrick started working out and playing sports. The activity helped Patrick to cope with the chaos around him. It helped him to survive the unpredictability, and it helped him to escape the chaos in his home life.

Patrick didn't talk about his feelings, and as he grew older, the only feeling he often felt was anger. If someone looked at him wrong, he would fly into a rage. Patrick had spent so many years suppressing and escaping his feelings that he wasn't in touch with his deep sadness and grief.

In his relationships, Patrick had a disorganized attachment style. He desired closeness, but he also feared it. When Patrick was 35 years old, he started therapy and began identifying his feelings. He started using the feelings wheel as a tool to stay in touch with his vulnerable feelings. This led to a path of healing for Patrick.

Taking Stock: Rating Your Emotions

REMEMBER

Before you can change how you react, you have to notice what you're feeling and how intensely you're feeling it.

Rating emotions is a tool that has developed across several psychological traditions over decades. Cognitive behavioral therapy (CBT) is the primary origin. In the 1970s, Aaron Beck and early CBT practitioners taught clients to name the emotion, rate its intensity, and track how the number changed after a new thought or behavior. In the 1990s, Marsha Linehan made emotion rating central to dialectical behavioral therapy (DBT). Clients would rate emotions to help them to identify them as well as to identify emotional triggers. Psychologists like James Gross and Paul Ekman studied emotional arousal using units of distress, arousal scales, and intensity ratings. Gottman therapy and emotional freedom technique (EFT) also have used numbers to help partners to identify the strength of their emotions. Rating emotions is a blended tool that is now widely used.

Rating your emotions helps you to manage or regulate them. When you rate them, you can notice if they're getting more or less intense. You can also notice that when you self-soothe, for example, the intensity of your emotions usually goes down. Rating gives you a gauge.

TIP

In the therapy room, I often have clients rate their emotions on a scale of 1 to 10, with 1 being the lowest and 10 being the highest. When people assign a number to their emotions, they're often surprised at their answer or their partners' answer.

EXAMPLE

Mario and Krista entered couples therapy to work on their relationship. Krista had an avoidant attachment style. When her nervous system became activated, she would shut down and pull away. She needed space and time to self-soothe. Mario had an anxious attachment. When he became emotionally flooded, he wanted to resolve things immediately. This would lead him to asking lots of questions and even making mild threats in session.

Mario and Krista were unaware of their attachment styles, their feelings, and what was happening internally. When Mario became flooded in session, I would notice by his facial expressions and his coloring. I asked Mario to pause, name his emotion, and rate it. He was able to express that he was feeling frustrated, and he rated his frustration at an intensity level of 7. Ten minutes later, after breathing and pausing, Sam was still at a 7. This gave Mario and Krista some information:

- It takes Mario a long time to move out of emotional flooding.
  - He floods quickly.
  - He needs more than just identification of feelings to deflood.

With time and practice, Mario started identifying and rating his emotions. Once he did, he could actively engage in an activity that lowered his intensity level and then return to a conversation with Krista.

You may be wondering what was happening to Krista when Mario was flooded. Typically, Krista was flooded too, but Mario didn't know it. Krista didn't show external signs of emotional flooding. The only sign was that she needed space. During session when I asked Krista to rate her emotions, she rated them a 5. This helped Mario to understand that Krista was physiologically flooded when she started to shut down. Both were able to learn how to rate their emotions and do what they needed to regulate them.

Regulating and Coregulating

You've probably seen the term *emotional regulation* everywhere — from social media posts to blogs and articles. It means:

- Noticing what you feel before it takes over
- Understanding how your body reacts to those feelings
- Being able to return to your baseline so that you can think clearly and act in line with your values

I often say to my clients that regulation is the process of creating a little bit of space between your emotional experience and your response.

Coregulation is another term often used. *Coregulation* is when another person, who can stay calm and present with you, helps you to regulate your emotions. Here's an example of coregulation:

- A parent, friend, or partner notices that you're getting overwhelmed.
- They respond with calm grounding behavior.
- Their steady presence helps your nervous system.

In short, regulation is how you manage yourself; coregulation is how others help you manage.

EXAMPLE

Janet and Phil often get stuck in the same argument, as many couples do. Janet is anxious attachment and Phil is disorganized (push-pull). When Janet feels distant or unheard, she gets hyperfocused on the relationship, worries intensely, and sometimes escalates emotionally. When Phil feels overwhelmed, he sometimes withdraws or shuts down, but other times, he can become reactive and defensive. In their typical argument, Janet notices tension rising and starts asking questions rapidly, trying to get reassurance. Phil feels flooded and pulls back or gets defensive, leaving Janet feeling more anxious. Janet and Phil entered couples therapy and began working on regulating and coregulating.

Now, instead of escalating, Janet notices her body's signals: racing heart, tight chest, and, most of all, her urge to interrupt. Phil notices his tension and tendency to get angry or shut down. Janet pauses and uses a grounding tool, usually deep breaths or a glass of ice water and a walk outside to self-soothe. Phil notices Janet's pause, and he chooses to stay present instead of pulling away. He offers a calm comment, such as, "Let's both take a breather and talk in 20 minutes."

REMEMBER

By each partner regulating themselves and supporting each other, the fight no longer spirals. Janet feels heard. Phil feels safe. They both feel loved and cared for.

Regulation tools

When you begin to experience strong feelings, you can use various tools to bring yourself back to a calmer state. In this section, I share some tools you can try using.

Breathing exercises

One common tool for helping an activated body settle is breathing exercises. There are many different techniques. Here I describe four options:

- **Deep breathing:** Slow steady breaths help signal to your nervous system that you're safe. Try inhaling for four counts, holding it for two, and exhaling for six.
- **Box breathing (square breathing):** Inhale for four counts, hold for four counts, exhale for four counts.
- **4-7-8:** Inhale for four counts, hold for seven counts, exhale for eight counts.
- **Belly breathing:** Place one hand on your chest and one on your belly. Breathe so your belly rises and falls while your chest stays mostly still.

Grounding exercises

Grounding is any technique that helps bring your attention back to the present moment. It works by connecting your body, senses, and surroundings. The following list includes several options:

- **5-4-3-2-1:** Check out your surroundings and notice the following things:
  - Five things you can see
  - Four things you can touch
  - Three things you can hear
  - Two things you can smell
  - One thing you can taste
- **Feet on the floor:** Take your shoes off and put your feet on the cool floor or cool grass or cement.
- **Movement grounding:** Walk slowly and notice each step. Roll your shoulders or stretch your arms. Try gently rocking or swaying.

Cold or warm sensation

Experiencing cold or warm sensations can either interrupt feelings of intense distress or create a sense of calm:

- Drink something warm or cool.
- Splash cold water on your face.
- Rub your hands together to generate warmth.
- Place a warm hand on your chest.

Putting It All Together: Quick Tools and Exercises

Here is a clear, step-by-step guide for you to identify and rate your emotions:

1. **Pause and take a moment to stop what you're doing.**
2. **Name the emotions.**
   - I feel frustrated.
   - I feel anxious.

3. **Rate the intensity of the emotion.**

- 1 = very mild/barely noticeable
- 5 = moderate/noticeable but manageable
- 10 = extreme/overwhelming

4. **Choose a quick regulation tool from the "Regulation tools" section.**

IN THIS CHAPTER

» Identifying how you feel and working with the five senses

» Embracing inner child work

» Using guided visualizations for healing

» Creating affirmations for grounding

Chapter 13

Healing Your Relationship with Yourself

When people who are struggling in their relationships come into my office, they often say things like, "My partner pulls away," "I feel constantly anxious in this relationship," or "I don't understand why I shut down during conflict." These patterns are very real and deserve attention. But in many cases, the emotional reactions people experience in adult relationships are connected to something that's been going on since before they became adults.

We call these *attachment wounds*, and they're expressed through anxious, avoidant, or disorganized patterns that typically develop earlier in life as ways of adapting to the emotional environment. If closeness felt unpredictable in your childhood, you may become highly sensitive to signs of distance or rejection. If emotional needs were discouraged or ignored, you may learn to rely heavily on yourself and feel uncomfortable depending on others. And if relationships were both comfortable and frightening at the same time, you may find yourself pulled between wanting connection and wanting to escape it.

Identifying What You're Feeling

Before you can heal attachment wounds, you first have to figure out how to recognize what you're feeling. In Chapter 12, I discuss why labeling emotions matters. If you'd like a refresher on how to identify emotions more clearly, you can revisit that chapter.

When people come into my office, they often describe feeling overwhelmed by anger, frustration, panic, or anxiety. These reactions can feel very intense in the body, such as a tight chest, racing thoughts, clenched muscles, or the urge to argue or shut down.

One of the first things I try to help people do is slow down and ask an important question:

> What emotion is underneath all of that activation?

Often, the surface reaction (anger, defensiveness, withdrawal) is covering a deeper feeling such as sadness, fear, or worry. When you can move past the physical surge of emotion and identify what you're truly feeling, you can begin to work with it.

Once a person can say something like "I feel hurt," "I'm scared," or "I'm worried about losing this relationship," they can begin building a plan to help them express themselves, cope with the feeling, and regulate their nervous system.

Let's look at an example.

EXAMPLE

Imagine Westley and Brooke have been together for three years. One evening, Brooke notices that Westley has been quiet and distracted. When she asks if something is wrong, he shrugs and says, "Nothing."

Brooke immediately feels a surge of frustration. Her thoughts start racing:

Why won't he just talk to me? He's shutting me out again. Maybe he doesn't care.

Before long, Brooke is raising her voice: "You never tell me what's going on! I'm tired of feeling like I'm the only one trying!"

From Westley's perspective, Brooke suddenly seems angry and critical. He shuts down even more, turning away and saying, "This is exactly why I don't say anything."

At first glance, Brooke's main emotion appears to be anger. But when I help her slow the moment down in therapy, something else often emerges. When Brooke pauses and pays attention to what she is feeling underneath the frustration, she might realize:

- I'm scared he's pulling away.
- I feel alone right now.
- I'm worried our relationship isn't okay.

Those emotions of fear, sadness, and worry are much more vulnerable than anger, but they're also much more useful to work with.

Instead of reacting with criticism, Brooke might learn to identify that what she's feeling is sadness, fear, and worry. When she can do this, she can say, "When you get quiet like that, I start to worry that something is wrong between us. I think I'm feeling scared right now."

That shift from reacting to identifying and expressing the deeper emotion is one of the first steps in healing attachment wounds.

Self-Soothing with the Five Senses

In Chapter 11, I discuss emotional flooding, which is when the body becomes overwhelmed by emotion and the nervous system goes into high alert. You can revisit that chapter if you'd like a deeper explanation. In this section, I talk about how to soothe yourself when that happens.

Many people enter therapy with attachment wounds already activated. In simple terms, activation means the nervous system has shifted into a stress response. Your body senses a possible emotional threat, such as rejection, criticism, distance, or conflict, and it reacts quickly.

When someone is activated, they may notice symptoms like the following:

- A racing heart
- Tightness in the chest or stomach
- Fast or scattered thoughts
- The urge to argue, defend, or shut down
- Feeling panicked, angry, or overwhelmed

REMEMBER

This reaction happens because the attachment system is designed to protect you. When a relationship feels unsafe or uncertain, your brain interprets it as a threat and prepares your body to respond. The problem is that when you're highly activated, the thinking part of your brain has a harder time doing its job. In other words, it becomes much more difficult to communicate clearly, listen well, or solve problems. That's why one of the most important skills in healing attachment wounds is learning how to ground yourself.

What is "grounding"

Grounding is simply helping your nervous system return to a calmer, more regulated state. Instead of staying stuck in your body's alarm response, grounding helps give your brain a signal that says, "You're safe enough to slow down."

When your body begins to settle, it becomes easier to identify your feelings, express them clearly, and respond thoughtfully rather than react impulsively.

One simple way to ground yourself is by using your five senses.

Using the five senses

The senses are powerful tools for calming your nervous system because they help bring your attention back to the present moment.

Here are a few ways you can use your senses to self-soothe when your feel activated:

- **Sight:** Look around the room and slowly name a few things you can see. Notice colors, shapes, or small details. This helps your brain shift away from racing thoughts and back into the present environment.
- **Touch:** Pay attention to physical sensations. You might hold a warm mug, wrap yourself in a blanket, press your feet into the floor, or place a hand on your chest while breathing slowly.
- **Sound:** Listen to something calming such as soft music, nature sounds, or the rhythm of your own breathing.
- **Smell:** Certain scents can signal safety to the brain. Many people find comfort in familiar smells such as lavender, peppermint, a favorite lotion, or even the scent of fresh coffee.
- **Taste:** Taking a slow sip of water or tea or noticing the flavor of something small like a mint, can also bring attention back into the body. Over time, practicing these grounding techniques can help you move from reacting automatically to responding more intentionally.

You may notice that grounding is not only helpful during moments of conflict with a partner but can help you take better care of yourself individually as well. When you learn how to calm your body and recognize what you're feeling, you become more capable of meeting your emotional needs. Instead of feeling completely overwhelmed by your reactions, you develop the ability to pause, understand what is happening inside you, and respond with more care toward yourself.

REMEMBER

This kind of self-awareness and self-regulation is an important part of healing attachment wounds. The more you learn to understand and soothe your emotional system, the more secure and steady you can begin to feel in your relationships with other people.

EXAMPLE

Allison is having a difficult conversation with her partner, Mickey. During the conversation, Mickey becomes quiet and pulls away. Almost immediately, Allison feels her body react. Her heart starts racing. Her chest feels tight, and her thoughts begin moving quickly. She feels a mix of panic, frustration, and anger.

Allison has a history of disorganized attachment, which means that moments of distance or conflict in relationships can quickly trigger feelings of fear and uncertainty. Even though part of her knows that Mickey may simply need a moment to think, her nervous system reacts as if something is very wrong.

Allison notices that she is becoming activated. Instead of continuing the conversation while feeling overwhelmed, she pauses and takes a moment to ground herself. She looks around the room and silently names five things she can see: the couch, a lamp, a picture on the wall, a window, and the coffee table. Next, Allison presses her feet into the floor and notices the feeling of the carpet beneath them. She takes a slow breath and places a hand on her chest. She listens for a few sounds in the room. She hears the hum of the air conditioner and the faint sound of traffic outside. After a minute or two, Allison notices that her breathing has slowed and her body feels a little calmer. Once she feels more regulated, Allison is better able to identify what she is feeling. Beneath the frustration, she realizes that she is feeling scared and worried about losing connection.

Getting to Know Your Inner Voice

An important part of healing attachment wounds involves learning to change the way you speak to yourself.

REMEMBER

When I talk about your inner voice, I'm referring to the fact that many people carry younger parts of themselves inside. These parts are often formed during earlier experiences in life and can still influence how you react in relationships today.

For example, someone might have a 5-year-old part that feels scared or worried about being abandoned. Another person might notice a 14-year-old part that becomes angry or shuts down when conflict arises. These younger parts are sometimes referred to as the *inner child*. They are not literally children living inside of a person, but they represent emotional experiences and coping strategies that developed earlier in life.

When attachment wounds are activated, these younger parts often speak the loudest through the inner voice. They may tell you that you aren't safe, that you're going to be rejected, or that you need to protect yourself by shutting down, arguing, or pulling away.

TIP

Part of healing involves learning to notice these inner voices with curiosity rather than criticism. When you can recognize that a younger part of you is feeling scared, hurt, or overwhelmed, you can begin responding with more understanding and care instead of reacting automatically.

Therapists have different ways of describing this process. Couples therapist Terry Real talks about moving from the "adaptive child" — the part that learned protective strategies earlier in life — to the "wise adult" — the part that can pause and respond thoughtfully. Other approaches, such as Internal Family Systems therapy, describe similar ideas using the language of "parts" inside a person. Regardless of the terminology, the goal is the same: learning to notice the younger reactive voice within us and developing a calmer, more compassionate voice to guide our responses.

EXAMPLE

Hailey has an anxious attachment style. In relationships, she tends to feel especially sensitive to signs that someone might be pulling away or becoming unavailable.

Her current relationship has been particularly challenging because her boyfriend struggles with addiction. When he's actively using substances, his behavior changes. He becomes more distant, less responsive, and sometimes unpredictable.

These moments can trigger deep activation for Hailey. Her body reacts quickly. Her thoughts start racing, and she feels scared and abandoned. Inside, her younger anxious part begins speaking loudly through her inner voice. She might think, *He doesn't care about me. I'm going to lose him. I have to do something to get his attention.*

When Hailey becomes this activated, she sometimes engages in what attachment researchers call protest behavior.

REMEMBER

Protest behavior refers to actions people take when they feel afraid of losing connection with someone important to them. These behaviors are often attempts, sometimes desperate ones, to restore closeness or reassurance. For a deeper discussion on protest behaviors, see Chapter 5.

For example, Hailey might send several texts in a row, repeatedly call her boyfriend, accuse him of not caring, or start an argument to get some kind of response. Although these behaviors come from a place of fear and longing for connection, they can sometimes push the other person further away, which only increases Hailey's anxiety.

Part of Hailey's healing involves learning to recognize when her anxious attachment system has been activated. When she can pause and notice the younger, fearful voice inside her, she can begin bringing in a more supportive and grounded inner voice.

Instead of reacting immediately, she might begin to tell herself, I'm feeling scared right now because this situation reminds me of past experiences of being left or hurt. I can take a moment to calm my body before deciding what to do.

REMEMBER

Figuring out how to notice and respond differently to these inner voices can help people like Hailey move out of automatic protest behaviors and toward healthier ways of coping with fear and uncertainty in relationships.

Beginning to change your inner voice

One of the most common reactions people have when they first hear about changing their inner voice is some version of, "Wait. Is this just positive thinking?"

REMEMBER

Changing your inner voice is not about pretending everything is fine or convincing yourself that life is perfect. Instead, it's about noticing when the voice inside your head has become overly harsh, critical, or fearful and knowing how to respond in a way that is more balanced, compassionate, and grounding.

In therapy, it's common to discover that the inner voice people carry today developed much earlier in life. It may echo the messages they heard growing up, the way others treated them, or the conclusions they formed about themselves or the world during painful experiences. Over time, those messages can turn into automatic thoughts. The goal of this work isn't to replace them with unrealistic positivity. The goal is to replace harsh self-judgment with a voice that is more truthful, steady, and supportive.

Once people understand this difference, they can begin practicing a few simple steps:

1. **Notice the voice.**
2. **Ask where the message came from.**
3. **Introduce a new voice.**
4. **Practice repeatedly.**

The following sections describe these steps.

Noticing the voice

Pay attention to what your inner voice says when you start to feel emotionally activated in a relationship. When your attachment system turns on, your inner voice may begin to predict danger in connection. You might hear thoughts like these:

- I'm being abandoned.
- They're going to leave me.
- Something is wrong with this relationship.
- I need to get their attention before they pull away.

Alternatively, the voice may sound more protective or distancing:

- This is too much.
- I'm going to be smothered.
- Being close means losing my freedom.
- I don't need anyone.
- I should handle this on my own.

TIP

In either case, the thoughts can feel extremely convincing in the moment, but often they're signals that the attachment system is activated rather than accurate reflections of what's happening in the present relationship.

Simply noticing these messages is an important first step. Many people have been hearing them for so long that they assume the thoughts are facts rather than automatic protective patterns.

Asking where the message came from

If you've been in therapy before, you may have heard questions like these:

- Where did that voice come from?
- Whose voice does that sound like?
- When did you first receive that message?

Your inner voice doesn't just appear out of nowhere. It's shaped over time through your relationships and experiences. Very often, the voice you hear in moments of distress is an echo of something you heard earlier in life.

It may come from a time when you felt vulnerable, scared, alone, rejected, or overwhelmed.

For example, the thought *I'm being abandoned* may trace back to moments where connection felt inconsistent or unpredictable. The belief *I'm going to be smothered* may come from experiences where closeness felt overwhelming or intrusive.

REMEMBER

When you begin to ask where the voice came from, you're getting to know your attachment wound and how to heal it.

EXAMPLE

Quentin and his girlfriend Gretta entered therapy after five years of dating. They enjoy an active life together of traveling, enjoying their garden and nurturing their animals. Quentin frequently gets scared of closeness in the relationship. When he does this, he pulls away temporarily. He later moves back toward Gretta. Quentin has a disorganized attachment style. His caregivers were overwhelming and unpredictable. When Quentin feels vulnerable, his inner voice says things like the following:

- It's time to go.
- I need space and freedom.
- I feel trapped.

Quentin's urge to leave makes more sense when viewed through the lens of his past. Growing up with caregivers who were overwhelming and unpredictable taught him that closeness could feel unsafe. As an adult, his inner voice still carries those old messages, interpreting vulnerability as a sign that he needs to escape or protect himself.

Introducing a new voice

TIP

Once you notice the old message, try responding with a more compassionate one. Imagine how you might speak to a close friend or to a younger version of yourself.

EXAMPLE

Using the example of Quentin and Gretta, Quentin's old inner voice possibly would have said, *I need to get out of here now*.

With conscious effort, Quentin can instead respond with a new inner voice that says something like:

- This was a hard moment. I can manage my emotions and stay present.
- It's okay to take a little space without shutting down completely.
- I don't have to choose between closeness and freedom. I can have both.

Notice the difference. The old voice is urgent and reactive. The new voice is grounding, flexible, and regulating.

Practicing repetition

Changing habits requires repetition, and altering your inner voice is no different. Each time you gently challenge the old message and replace it with a more balanced one, you're strengthening a new mental pathway.

Once you have identified the old message, understand where it comes from, and have created a more balanced response, the next step is practice. When you feel triggered, intentionally repeat your new message to yourself. Over time, this helps strengthen new neural pathways and makes the new voice feel more natural. Here are some examples:

- I'm feeling scared and disconnected right now.
- This feeling is familiar. It doesn't mean I'm actually being abandoned.
- I can pause before reacting.
- I am worthy of love and consistency.
- I can ask for what I need in a clear and grounded way.
- I don't have to chase connection. I can create it differently.

REMEMBER

The old voice is panicked, urgent, and fear-based. The new voice is soothing, steady, and self-supportive.

Rewriting your inner voice

I do an exercise with many of my clients in which I ask them to think about a recent situation where they felt activated in a relationship: anxious, shut down, overwhelmed, or reactive. This is an exercise you can try with your own recent situation:

1. **Identify your old voice.**

   What did your inner voice say in that moment? Write down a few of the thoughts you had while the situation was occurring. For example,

   - I'm being abandoned.
   - I need to get out of here.
   - I'm too much.
   - They don't really care about me.

2. **Get curious about your voice's origin.**

   Consider where that voice came from. Ask yourself

   - Where have I felt this before?
   - When did I first learn this message?
   - Whose voice does this sound like?

3. **Create a new voice.**

   Think of a different way you can respond to that same type of moment from a more grounded, compassionate place. What could your new inner voice say? What would a kinder inner voice say? How could your new inner voice acknowledge your feelings while still being compassionate? What would a grounded inner voice say?

   For example,

   - I'm feeling scared right now, but that doesn't mean I'm being abandoned.
   - I can take space without completely shutting down.
   - I'm allowed to have needs, and I can express them calmly.
   - This feeling will pass. I don't have to react immediately.

4. **Practice in real time.**

   The next time you feel activated, see if you can gently introduce this new voice. At first, it may feel unnatural or even unconvincing, and that's okay. It takes time to create a new inner voice. Be patient with yourself and with your process. You're practicing a new way of relating to yourself.

REMEMBER

Your old inner voice developed for a reason. It was shaped by experiences where you were doing the best you could to feel safe, connected, or protected. Changing your inner voice isn't about criticizing those old patterns. It's about offering yourself something new.

Taking Care of Your Whole Self: Working with Your Inner Child

At the heart of healing your relationship with yourself is something often referred to as *inner child work*. It simply means recognizing that parts of you, especially the emotional, reactive parts, were shaped much earlier in life, and are still influencing how you feel, think, and respond today.

Understanding your inner child

Most people carry younger versions of themselves inside. This inner child might be one of the following:

- A younger part that feels scared of being left
- A part that learned to shut down when things felt overwhelming
- A part that tries hard to keep others close or keep the peace

REMEMBER

These parts developed for a reason. At one point, they were adaptive. They helped you navigate your environment, your relationships, and your emotional world. In adulthood, though, those same responses can sometimes feel confusing, intense, or out of proportion to the present moment.

TIP

Have you ever had a reaction that felt bigger than the situation? For example:

- You felt panicked when someone didn't text back.
- You shut down during a difficult conversation.
- You felt overwhelmed by closeness or conflict.

In those moments, it's often your inner child stepping forward. Instead of judging yourself in these moments, use curiosity to ask yourself *What does this part of me need right now?* Listen to the answer. For example:

- *I'm feeling scared right now, and I need reassurance and connection. What can I do to take care of myself right now?*
- *This reminds me of something older. This isn't actually about my partner. I need some time to calm down and ground myself.*
- *I don't have to handle this the way I used to. I can ask for what I need directly.*

Reparenting yourself

Inner child work is sometimes called *reparenting*. It means learning to give yourself what you may not have consistently received in the past, such as reassurance, safety, validation, boundaries, and emotional support.

For example, when you feel the following things, you can "parent" yourself by responding in a way that you didn't experience when you were younger:

» When you feel abandoned, tell yourself, *I'm here. I'm not leaving you.*

» When you feel overwhelmed, reassure yourself.

» When you feel like you're "too much," remind yourself, *your needs and feelings make sense.*

Reparenting also means recognizing that parts of your 5-year-old, 10-year-old, or 15-year-old self may still carry unmet needs. Caregivers are human, so even well-meaning caregivers can miss things, especially if they were navigating their own stress, limitations, or unresolved wounds. In some cases, caregivers were emotionally unavailable or even harmful. The result is that certain parts of the self may have gone unsupported or were shaped in ways that required you to adapt so that you could cope.

REMEMBER

Reparenting is the process of going back and tending to those parts now with more awareness, intention, and care than may have been possible at the time.

EXAMPLE

Peyton grew up in a home where emotions weren't openly talked about. When she was upset, she was often told she was "overreacting" or encouraged to move on quickly. No one was intentionally trying to harm her, but there wasn't much space for her emotional world.

As an adult, Peyton notices that when something feels off in her relationship, like a delayed text or a change in tone, her system reacts quickly. She feels anxious and unsettled, and she has the urge to reach out repeatedly or seek reassurance. At other times, she swings the opposite way and tells herself to "just not care."

Before she worked on understanding her attachment style and self-soothing, Peyton's inner voice said things like this:

- *You're too much.*
- *Don't make this a big deal.*
- *If you need too much, people will leave.*

Through reparenting, Peyton started to respond to herself differently. When she noticed her anxiety rising, instead of immediately reacting, she started pausing and checking in internally:

- *Something here feels scary. That makes sense.*
- *I don't have all the information yet. I can slow this down.*
- *Even if this doesn't go the way I want, I can handle it.*

Over time, Peyton became more thoughtful in how she responded, rather than automatically reacting. Through this work, she learned how to take good care of herself.

EXAMPLE

Alec didn't grow up in a consistently stable emotional environment. Some days his caregivers felt connected and easy. Other days, they were tense, unpredictable, or emotionally distant. Over time, he learned two things at once:

- Connection feels good.
- Connection isn't always safe.

Now, in his relationship with Tanya, Alec's past experiences show up as a push–pull pattern. At the beginning, things felt natural. Alec was engaged, attentive, and present. Tanya responded well to this. She felt close to him, and the relationship started to build. But after a few weeks of consistent closeness, something shifts internally for Alec.

One night, Tanya sent a simple text: "I miss you today. Want to come over later?"

Alec read it and instead of feeling good, he felt pressure. His thoughts began to shift: *This is getting to be a lot. I need some space. I don't want to feel tied down.* So he didn't respond right away. After a few hours passed, he wrote something brief: "Busy tonight. Maybe another time."

From Tanya's perspective, the response was confusing. Just the day before, Alec seemed fully in. Now he seemed distant. She replied, "Okay . . . everything alright?"

Alec sees the message, and a different part of him activates. He feels a flicker of anxiety: *Did I just mess this up? Why does this feel off now? I don't want her to pull away.*

So he shifts again. This time moving back toward connection, and he replies, "Yeah, just had a long day. I can come by for a bit."

To Tanya, this feels inconsistent. To Alec, it feels confusing. Internally, he's moving among different states: wanting closeness before needing distance and then fearing the distance.

Through his reparenting work in therapy, Alec begins to recognize what's happening inside him. The next time a similar moment happens, he pauses. Instead of immediately pulling away, he checks in with himself: *Part of me feels pressure right now. That doesn't automatically mean I need to shut this down.*

Instead of swinging all the way back when anxiety hits, he thinks, *I can feel uncomfortable without fixing this immediately.*

He learns to respond more steadily and replies, "I've had a long day and might need a low-key night, but I'd still like to see you." Over time, this changes the pattern. Tanya experiences a more consistent Alec, who feels less controlled by the internal push-pull. Reparenting, for Alec, means learning how to tolerate closeness without feeling trapped and tolerate space without feeling abandoned.

Using Guided Imagery

Guided imagery is a simple but powerful way to help your nervous system settle and feel safer. It involves visualizing safe places, spaces, or scenarios to calm your mind and body. Many therapists incorporate guided imagery into their work with clients. Research shows that guided imagery reduces anxiety, helps with physical pain and tension, and improves nervous system regulation. It's also used improve sleep because it relaxes the mind and the body.

TECHNICAL STUFF

Clinical studies have found that guided imagery can reduce anxiety, improve physiological markers of stress like heart rate and decrease perceived pain. It's a low risk, evidence-supported way to help the body shift out of stress.

TIP

When you have attachment wounds, your body may react as if you're still in an unsafe or unpredictable environment even when you're not. Guided imagery gives your system a new experience: one of safety, steadiness, and support. Over time, this can soften automatic reactions associated with attachment wounds.

One of the nice things about guided imagery is that you can do it anywhere. You don't need anything fancy. You can be in your bedroom, your office, your living room, or any quiet space.

Follow these steps:

1. **Get comfortable.**

   Sit or lie down in a position where your body can relax — even just a little.

2. **Slow your breathing.**

   Take a few slow, steady breaths. Begin to notice your inhale and exhale. Take a breath in through your nose and out through your mouth while focusing on a long exhale. Continue breathing slowly until your body begins to relax. You may feel your shoulders drop and your jaw soften.

   TIP

   A longer exhale helps calm your body. While breathing in slightly activates your system, breathing out tells it to slow down. Extending your exhale, even by a couple of seconds, is one of the fastest ways to reduce stress in the moment.

3. **Create a safe scene.**

   Imagine a place where you feel calm, steady, or at ease. Here are some examples:

   - A beach at sunset
   - A quiet room with soft lighting
   - The mountains
   - Sitting on a porch with someone you trust
   - In a completely imagined place

   Try to engage your senses:

   - What do you see?
   - What do you hear?
   - What does the air feel like?
   - What is it like to be in this place?

   TIP

   If you're working with affirmations, which I explain in the next section, this is a good place to add some affirmations while you're breathing and visualizing yourself in a safe place where you're at ease.

4. **Add support.**

   If it feels right, imagine a supportive presence there with you. This could be

   - A trusted person
   - A version of your older, wiser self
   - A steady, calm figure who simply sits with you

5. **Linger for a moment in this safe scene.**

   Let yourself stay in that scene for a minute or two. If your mind wanders, gently bring it back.

EXAMPLE

Billy, who often feels trapped in close relationships, notices his body tightening during conflict with his partner. He begins practicing guided imagery by picturing himself sitting by a quiet lake with space around him and no pressure to respond. Instead of feeling cornered, he begins to feel a sense of choice and breathing room. Over time, this helps him stay more present during real conversations so he doesn't shut down or pull away.

Grounding Affirmations for the Self

In my clinical practice, I have used affirmations often with clients who are working on healing attachment wounds. An *affirmation* is a statement that you say to yourself to influence your thoughts, emotions, and behavior.

TECHNICAL STUFF

Research shows that realistic, believable self-talk — often called *self-affirmation* — can reduce stress, lower defensiveness, and help people stay more grounded under pressure. The key is that the statement needs to feel true enough for the brain to accept it. For example, if a client feels down on themselves about getting a C on a test, the affirmation shouldn't be, "I am great at taking math tests." A more realistic affirmation might be, "I am working hard" or "I am on a learning curve. I am improving my score slowly."

Making an affirmation "grounding"

A grounding affirmation has the following qualities:

- It feels realistic (not exaggerated).
- It helps your body settle, even slightly.
- It speaks to what you need.

TIP

Grounding affirmations can be either broad, all-purpose reminders or specific statements designed for situations that tend to trigger you. Many people find that the most effective affirmations are tailored to the feelings, fears, or challenges they experience most often. You can think of affirmations as supportive statements.

EXAMPLE

Here are some examples of grounding affirmations:

- When you feel anxious or afraid of abandonment:
  - I'm feeling scared, but I can take good care of myself through this.
  - This feeling will pass, even if it's uncomfortable right now.
- When you feel overwhelmed or flooded:
  - I can slow this down.
  - I don't have to figure everything out at once.
- When you feel the urge to shut down or pull away:
  - I can take space without disappearing.
  - I don't have to do this alone.

Using grounding affirmations

You can incorporate affirmations into your healing in lots of different ways. Here are some options:

- Pick one that fits what you're feeling
- Say it slowly (out loud or in your head)
- Use them in your artwork
- Write them in a journal or in the notes section of your phone for triggering moments
- Go over them once a day
- Include them in a guided visualization exercise as descried in the "Using Guided Imagery" section earlier in this chapter

REMEMBER

It's important that your affirmation speaks to you. Work with the wording and explore different wording until it works for you.

IN THIS CHAPTER

» Considering others' attachment styles

» Pausing before you react

» Planning to practice regulation

» Watching for attachment triggers in your day-to-day routine

» Balancing closeness and separation

Chapter 14

Healing Your Relationship with Others

For a long time, the message that many of us received was that if you had attachment issues, you needed to work on yourself and then come back into relationships. Although that is certainly true for some, that idea doesn't capture the whole picture.

Attachment wounds don't form in isolation. They form in relationships. Consequently, you don't fully heal them by yourself, either. They heal while you're in the middle of interactions, when you're triggered, when things feel uncertain, and when you have the chance to respond differently than you have in the past. This chapter is about figuring out how to work with your attachment patterns when in relationships with other people.

Keeping Others' Attachment Styles in Mind

In my work with individuals and couples, I often see people who feel triggered or frustrated by their partner's reactions. They may quickly conclude that their partner doesn't care, is pulling away, or is rejecting them. What's usually missing is context. Each person brings into the relationship their own attachment history that's affected by early experiences, past relationships, and how their nervous system learned to handle closeness, distance, and stress. In other words, in a relationship with another person, the partner isn't reacting the way you would. They're reacting based on their own wiring.

The differences between two people in a relationship tend to show up most clearly during moments of distress, conflict, or high emotional need. When you don't take that into account, it's easy to misinterpret what's happening and react in ways that escalate the situation. Understanding someone else's attachment style doesn't mean excusing harmful behavior. It means accurately interpreting what's happening so you can respond more effectively instead of reacting automatically.

Understanding attachment offers a different lens for interpreting how people react. Without this lens, behavior can feel confusing or even hurtful. With it, behavior becomes more understandable.

EXAMPLE

Charlie feels anxious when Elena pulls away after an argument. After conflict, he texts, "Are we okay? Why aren't you answering?" Elena, feeling overwhelmed, takes space. She thinks, *I just need a minute to breathe.*

Charlie experiences her silence as abandonment. Elena experiences his messages as pressure. Both feel misunderstood.

EXAMPLE

Rosa and Natalia have been close friends for years. They usually text daily and share details about their lives. Recently, Natalia went through a stressful reorganization at work. She suddenly stopped initiating texts and gave one-word answers. Because Rosa understands how Natalia tends to cope, she is able to convey understanding and empathy. She sends a low-pressure text that says, "Hey, I know you're drowning at work right now. Just wanted you to know that I love you and am here for you. We can talk whenever things calm down for you."

EXAMPLE

Casandra and Val are sisters. They've been through a lot together through the years, with lots of ups and downs, but they're now at a pretty stable place in their relationship. Casandra likes to talk regularly about her day, and although Val enjoys it, her life is extremely busy. Val deals with stress by hyperfocusing on the things that need to be done. Over the years, Casandra has tended to experience this as rejection. It sometimes has caused arguments between the two sisters. What has helped their relationship is understanding each other's stress response.

Relationship therapists call this *attunement*. Val has grown to know that Casandra can easily feel rejected. When she senses this, she often reaches out and says, "Hey, I'm not ignoring you. I'm just feeling very overwhelmed right now, but I'd love to hang out on Saturday."

REMEMBER

People's reactions are often about regulation, not rejection. When you begin to recognize these patterns, you're less likely to immediately personalize what's happening and instead understand that the other person is also trying to process emotions. Instead of thinking, "They don't care about me," you might begin to think, "They may be overwhelmed right now." That shift can change your response.

Stopping Before You React: Practicing the Pause

When I watch attachment reactions unfold in real time in my office, one thing stands out every time: They show up in the body before the mind has time to make sense of them because attachment reactions are fast.

If you pay close attention, you will likely notice physiological symptoms. Your chest tightens, your breathing changes, your thoughts speed up, or you feel an immediate urge to say something, fix something, or get away. Before you've had time to think it through, you're already reacting. That's because these responses aren't just thoughts. They're nervous system patterns. If you don't slow things down, you end up responding from that automatic place and escalating, shutting down, or moving into old patterns that don't actually help.

REMEMBER

Pausing is what interrupts that cycle. Even a few seconds can create enough space to respond more intentionally instead of reacting on autopilot.

EXAMPLE

Simone notices her partner hasn't responded in a few hours. Her mind jumps to *He's losing interest*.

Her usual pattern is to send multiple texts or withdraw. This time, she pauses. She puts down her phone and tells herself, *I'm activated right now. I don't actually know what's going on*. She calls a friend and goes for a walk.

Later, her partner responds that he had been in meetings all day.

TIP

If you feel urgency, there's a good chance that it's a result of *activation*. We use this word to describe what happens when you're nervous system is in arousal. Read more about activation in Chapter 11.

REMEMBER

When you pause, it gives you space to choose what to do next.

Becoming Intentional: Having a Plan

When people begin working on attachment healing, there are two parts to the process: developing awareness and learning to respond differently. Awareness helps you recognize your patterns and understand where they come from. When you're triggered, something other than rational thought takes over. Your body becomes activated, your thinking narrows, and you're much more likely to fall back into old, familiar reactions even if they don't help you or reflect who you want to be. That's why having a plan of how to respond differently can be so powerful.

In my work with individuals and couples, I've found that when people know what they want to do in those moments and when they've practiced it, they're much more able to interrupt the pattern and respond in a healthier way.

To develop a plan, ask yourself these questions:

- What do I usually do when I feel disconnected?
- How do I usually handle it if I feel fear of being smothered or fear of abandonment?
- What would I like to do instead?
- How do I want to handle it next time I feel triggered or activated?
- How can I take care of myself in these moments?
- What helps to calm me down or bring me back to baseline?

EXAMPLE

Chris tends to shut down during conflict. He did some work in therapy and was able to identify what he needs when he's feeling like shutting down. He discovered that he needs to take a break instead of withdrawing without warning.

Chris develops a plan to communicate to his partner ahead of time before he is shut down. When his partner says, "We need to talk," Chris usually feels overwhelmed and withdraws.

Instead of disappearing, Chris begins practicing to say, "I want to have this conversation. I just need 10 minutes to get grounded." This small shift allows him to re-engage without becoming flooded.

REMEMBER

Planning ahead gives you something to return to when emotions run high.

Committing to Regulating Yourself

When I talk about *regulating emotions*, I'm referring to the way you manage emotions. Much of my work with couples involves teaching regulation skills. In fact, I often tell couples that once we build a solid foundation of regulation, everything else becomes more workable. Conversations improve. Conflict becomes less overwhelming. People feel less reactive and more in control. Regulation is essential and is the foundation of good communication.

At its core, regulation is your ability to manage your emotional and physical responses in the moment, especially when something feels upsetting, threatening, or overwhelming. Without it, even small issues can escalate quickly. With it, you have more space to think, communicate, and stay connected.

REMEMBER

If your body is overwhelmed, it's much harder to listen, communicate clearly, and stay present.

Regulation doesn't mean you don't react. It means you can stay grounded enough to respond.

EXAMPLE

Aria feels overwhelmed when her partner becomes frustrated. Her body reacts immediately with a tightening of her chest and racing thoughts. Instead of reacting defensively, she slows her breathing, grounds her feet, and thinks *I'm safe enough right now*. (Read more about these techniques in Chapter 13.) She stays present instead of shutting down.

EXAMPLE

Nadia and Saanvi get home after an exhausting day. Nadia is pacing and frustrated by a difficult project. Saanvi is feeling overwhelmed by work and emails. In the past, this type of situation led to an argument. Saanvi used to withdraw, causing Nadia to feel abandoned, and Nadia used to vent anxiously, making Saanvi feel more overwhelmed. They both have done work in therapy to recognize that they are in a stress response. They have committed to a plan to notice when they are overwhelmed and have a plan to self-soothe. They use a code word to indicate that they are both at their threshold. Saanvi tells Nadia he is going to take the dog for a walk, and Nadia takes a bath. Both of their nervous systems settle, and they reconvene an hour later.

REMEMBER

Over time, regulation becomes more accessible and automatic.

Noticing Attachment Triggers in Daily Life

Attachment triggers don't just show up in the big, obvious moments. They show up in the small, everyday interactions that most people overlook. I see this all the time in my office. It can be something as simple as a shift in tone, not getting a text back, feeling left out, your partner needing space, or even feeling like someone is coming toward you with too much intensity or need. Suddenly, something in you reacts. You might feel anxious, rejected, pressured, or like you need to pull away, and it can happen so fast you don't even fully register it at first.

These moments may seem small on the surface, but they're not small to your nervous system. They're tapping into older attachment experiences, and before you know it, you're reacting from an old place.

EXAMPLE

Ming notices his partner is quieter than usual. His mind jumps to *Did I do something wrong?*

Instead of reacting immediately, Ming pauses and asks, "Hey, you seem a little off. Is everything okay?"

His partner replies, "I'm just tired," and the situation settles before it escalates.

REMEMBER

Not every feeling is a signal of danger. Recognizing triggers early gives you more flexibility in how you respond.

Navigating Closeness and Space

Over the years of working with couples, I've found myself coming back to the same idea again and again: In a healthy relationship, there is an I, a we, and a you. Every person needs space to be themselves to have their own interests, friendships, and time alone, but everyone also needs to nurture their relationships with their partners — that shared space where the relationship feels protected and prioritized.

Where this gets tricky, and where I see couples get stuck all the time, is in balancing closeness and space. The truth is, not all people need the same amount of each. One partner may crave more connection, more time together, ad more reassurance, whereas the other may need more room to breathe, more independence, and more time to themselves. This difference isn't just about preference. It's about attachment.

REMEMBER

Closeness and space are deeply tied to your attachment history. For someone with more anxious attachment, closeness often feels like safety. Distance can feel like danger, even when nothing is actually wrong. For someone with more avoidant attachment, space often feels regulating. Too much closeness can feel overwhelming, like a loss of autonomy or pressure to show up in ways that feel uncomfortable. So what looks like a simple difference — "You want more time together than I do" — is often something much deeper. It's about what your nervous system experiences as safe or unsafe.

Examining a common pattern

Let's take a look at how quickly differences in needs can play out.

EXAMPLE

Lauren starts to notice that Danny has been quieter in the evenings. He's on his phone more and less engaged. After a few days, Lauren says, "Are we okay?"

Danny, who has had a long day and is feeling mentally drained, responds, "Yeah, I'm just tired. I think I just need some time to decompress."

Lauren hears, *He's pulling away.*

Danny's experience is, *I can't even have a minute to myself.*

Lauren moves closer, asking more questions, trying to reconnect, and looking for reassurance. Danny pulls back further with short answers, less eye contact, and more withdrawal.

Within minutes, they're in a cycle. Lauren feels anxious and rejected. Danny feels pressured and overwhelmed. Neither of them is wrong. They're just managing closeness and space in opposite ways.

Understanding what's actually happening

In a situation like Lauren and Danny's, a few important things are happening under the surface:

- One partner experiences distance as disconnection or abandonment.
- The other experiences closeness as pressure or overwhelm.
- Both partners react quickly, often before they've even named what they feel.
- The behaviors that follow (pursuing or withdrawing) reinforce the cycle.

Breaking down why this feels so intense

Part of what makes this dynamic so challenging is how fast it happens. The reactions are not slow and logical By the time you're aware of what's happening, you may already be in it, pushing for connection or pulling away to create space. Because these reactions are tied to earlier attachment experiences, they often feel bigger than the moment itself, for example,

- A delayed response isn't just a delayed response. It often feels like rejection.
- A request for space isn't just a request. It can feel like disconnection or abandonment.

When you understand this, it becomes easier to step out of blame and into awareness.

REMEMBER

Needing closeness doesn't make you "too much." Needing space doesn't make you "not enough." Everyone has different attachment needs.

Finding ways to navigate closeness and space

Differences in how people approach closeness and space are a normal part of relationships. The goal isn't to eliminate those differences but to understand them. When partners can recognize and communicate their needs, they're better able to stay connected even when their needs aren't the same.

Here are some ways to navigate these situations:

- **Talk about needs before you're triggered.** These conversations go much better when you're calm, not in the middle of a reaction.
- **Be clear and specific.** Saying, "I need 20 minutes to decompress," is very different from shutting down or walking away without explanation.
- **Reassure when you take space.** A simple, "I'm not going anywhere. I just need a little time," can make a big difference.
- **Don't immediately personalize your partner's behavior.** Their need for space or closeness is often about the way they regulate their emotions.
- **Work on your own regulation (self-soothing skills).** The more regulated you are, the less extreme these moments will feel. Read more about self-soothing in Chapter 13.

» **Ask yourself the following questions:**

- What is this situation bringing up for me?
- What can I do to take care of myself right now?
- When do I tend to want more closeness?
- When do I tend to want more space?
- What do I tell myself in those moments?
- What assumptions do I make about my partner?

TIP

When you're calm, take some time to reflect on your typical reactions to closeness and space. Understanding your patterns ahead of time can help you respond more intentionally the next time attachment needs or relationship stress arise.

Putting It All Together

Healing your relationship with others isn't about getting it right every time. It's about

» Understanding what's happening beneath the surface

» Slowing down your reactions

» Responding with more intention

» Regulating yourself in difficult moments

» Sharing feelings and communicating clearly

REMEMBER

Every time you pause instead of react, you're changing something. Every time you respond differently, you're creating a new pattern. Over time, those patterns shape your relationships into something more stable, more connected, and more secure.

When two partners want opposite things at the same time

There's another dynamic I want to name because it can feel confusing. Sometimes, it's not just that one partner wants closeness and the other wants space. Sometimes, both partners want these things, but they want them at different times. This is often the case with disorganized or push-pull patterns.

EXAMPLE

Mayu deeply wants connection. She wants to feel close, chosen, and prioritized. But when Kevin gets too close — asking a lot of questions and wanting to talk things through — she starts to feel overwhelmed and shuts down.

Kevin also wants closeness. But when Mayu pulls away, something in him gets activated. He moves toward her, tries harder, asks more, and pushes for connection. The more he moves in, the more she pulls back. The more she pulls back, the more he moves in.

But when Kevin eventually gets frustrated and backs off? Mayu starts to feel anxious. Now she wants closeness again.

This is what we see with disorganized attachment. It's a push-pull dynamic that can feel exhausting for both partners. They both want connection, but their nervous systems don't feel safe in it at the same time. For more on disorganized attachment, read Chapter 7.

In patterns like this, you see the following conditions:

- Both partners may fear disconnection and feel overwhelmed by closeness.
- The timing of their needs doesn't match.
- Each person's coping strategy triggers activation in the other.

This can create a cycle that feels confusing and even chaotic.

Handling push-pull dynamics

The push-pull dynamic can be difficult to navigate. Try some of the following techniques for handling them in your relationships:

- **Slow the cycle down.** You may say to yourself, *We're getting caught in our push pull cycle again*, or say to your partner, "I think we're stuck in our usual pattern right now." Acknowledging it directly in this way can create enough space to respond differently.
- **Work on tolerating small amounts of discomfort.** Closeness might feel like too much. Space might feel like too much. Growth happens in small, manageable stretches.
- **Communicate mixed needs.** It's okay to say, "Part of me wants to be close, and part of me feels overwhelmed."

» **Focus on safety, not perfection.** The goal isn't to get it exactly right. It's to create more emotional safety over time.

Putting this techniques into practice

The work of navigating closeness and space isn't about eliminating differences. Those differences will always be there. The goal is to understand them, talk about them, and respond to them in a way that builds connection instead of breaking it down. When couples can do this and when they can recognize the pattern, regulate themselves, and communicate clearly, something shifts. Closeness feels safer, and the sense of safety feels less threatening. Partners begin to understand each other and they learn how to navigate space and closeness in a way that works for both parties.

IN THIS CHAPTER

- » **Emotional safety and creating it in relationships**
- » **Getting to know the couple bubble**
- » **Repairing relationships**
- » **Building emotional attunement in a relationship**

Chapter 15 Building Safety

When I work with couples in my practice, one of the first questions I help them explore is, "Is there safety in our relationship?"

When safety is present, couples can grow, change, and begin working on deeper layers like intimacy, connection, and shared dreams. Without safety, those things are almost impossible to build. In many ways, this mirrors the idea behind Maslow's Hierarchy of Needs, which is the idea that people need a sense of basic security before they can reach for higher levels of growth. You need a roof over your head before you can focus on self-esteem, and relationships need emotional safety before they can thrive.

When there is safety in a relationship, partners can be vulnerable and open, and they can move through conflict without losing connection. When safety feels uncertain, even small moments can trigger strong reactions such as defensiveness, withdrawal, or escalation.

Safety is built through consistent, predictable experiences of being understood, responded to, and emotionally held. This chapter focuses on how couples actively build safety by showing up for each other again and again.

Looking at Emotional Safety

Emotional safety is the felt sense that you can be open, vulnerable, and real with your partner without fear of being dismissed, attacked, or shut out.

It doesn't mean there's no conflict or that everything is always calm. It means that even when things are hard, you trust that the relationship can hold together because your partner will stay engaged, responsive, and respectful.

When emotional safety is present, partners can say what they feel without immediately bracing for a negative reaction. They can express needs, admit mistakes, and stay in the conversation even when emotions are high. There's a sense that the relationship is stable enough to handle discomfort.

Before I share how couples build safety, it's important to understand how easily safety can be disrupted. I see many different ways that safety gets broken down in everyday interactions.

Recognizing how safety breaks in everyday moments

Safety in a relationship can easily be disrupted. In this section, I give you a few examples of what that can look like.

EXAMPLE

Becca shared with Simon that she was feeling smothered, and Simon dismissed her experience. In that moment, Becca's vulnerability wasn't met with understanding.

Cassie asked Darius to prioritize their relationship, and Darius responded with defensiveness and criticism. What started as a request for connection quickly turned into disconnection.

Tony asked Katherine to consider his feelings about her contact with an ex, and Katherine shut down for days and left the home. Tony felt abandoned.

Mason deeply cared about Dominique, but he experienced her repeated crossing of his boundaries as overwhelming. What felt like closeness to her began to feel unsafe and invasive to him.

In each of these moments, a partner is reaching out, and the response they receive impacts whether they feel safe.

When safety is missing, the dynamic shifts quickly. Partners become protective. One may pursue, trying to get a response or reassurance. The other may withdraw, trying to avoid conflict or overwhelm. Conversations escalate or shut down, not because the issue is unsolvable, but because the relationship no longer feels like a safe place.

REMEMBER

Most couples assume safety comes from resolving problems or improving communication skills. In reality, safety is built through repeated experiences of responsiveness, how partners show up for each other in small, everyday moments. It's not created in one conversation. It's created over time, through consistency.

REMEMBER

Before couples can change their patterns or resolve deeper issues, safety has to be established. Without it, even the best tools won't stick. With it, partners can begin to move out of protection and deepen their connection.

Understanding emotional safety as an attachment experience

Emotional safety isn't just created through communication skills or good intentions; its rooted in attachment. At its core, safety comes from the experience of knowing that your partner is there for you in a meaningful and consistent way.

According to Dr. Sue Johnson, the developer of Emotionally Focused Therapy (EFT), partners are constantly asking three questions:

- Are you there for me?
- Do I matter to you?
- Will you respond when I reach for you?

REMEMBER

These questions aren't always spoken out loud. Sometimes they're implied and present in the background rather than being outwardly stated.

When they answer feels like "yes," your nervous system settles. When they answer feels uncertain or like "no," the nervous system shifts into protection.

TIP

According to attachment theory, emotional safety is built through three core experiences: accessibility, responsiveness, and engagement.

- **Accessibility:** Are you there for me? Can I reach you emotionally or do you shut down, withdraw or turn away?

- **Responsiveness:** Will you respond when I reach? When I share something vulnerable, do you acknowledge me, dismiss me, or defend yourself?
- **Engagement:** Do I matter to you? Do I feel important, valued, and emotionally connected to you?

It's important to understand that these needs apply to all partners — even those who tend to shut down or withdraw.

REMEMBER

For more avoidant or withdrawn partners, accessibility, responsiveness, and engagement can feel more complicated. Closeness may feel overwhelming. Emotional intensity may feel like pressure. But underneath that withdrawal is often a different way of managing the same questions, such as

- Is it safe to stay present right now?
- Will I be overwhelmed if I engage?
- Is there space for me in this relationship?

REMEMBER

As partners begin to experience consistent, nonthreatening connection, even those who tend to withdraw can begin to

- Stay present a little longer
- Respond a little more openly
- Feel safer engaging over time

EXAMPLE

Gina and Omari had been dating for a year. Gina has kids. Omari met her kids and started to build a friendly relationship with them. Gina was very protective of her children because of some things in their history. Gina was on guard about anyone correcting them. Omari steered clear of correcting the kids, and he knew that his role in their lives was not to parent.

One day, Gina's son disrespected Omari. Omari made the choice to tell him that it was disrespectful. Gina had a strong reaction to it. In the past this would have triggered Gina's avoidant attachment style and she would have shut down and pulled away.

Now that Gina understood that her urge to shut down was being driven by old attachment wounds and protective instincts, she was able to make a different decision. Omari and Gina sat down together and had a discussion. Gina described the events that occurred in the past that made this situation triggering for her. Omari heard her. Omari described how he felt when her son disrespected him. Gina heard and understood him. They both felt truly seen by each other, and they were able to have future conversations that helped them to problem-solve more. However, the initial conversations were about hearing and understanding each other.

Evaluating the structure of emotional safety

Emotional safety doesn't happen by accident. It's built over time through consistent patterns in the ways partners relate to each other day to day. Research by John Gottman, a psychologist and relationship researcher known for his decades of work studying couples, shows that strong, stable relationships share certain foundational elements that support trust, connection, and resilience.

REMEMBER

These foundational elements don't eliminate conflict. They change how people experience conflict.

TIP

When the following elements are present, partners are more likely to feel secure, valued, and understood. When they're missing, even small interactions can begin to feel threatening:

- **Trust:** The belief that your partner is emotionally reliable and that they will respond, consider your needs, and act in ways that support the relationship
- **Commitment:** A shared sense that the relationship matters and is worth protecting, even during difficult moments
- **Turning toward (responding to bids for connection):** The everyday ways partners respond to each other's attempts for attention, support, or connection
- **Fondness and admiration:** A foundation of respect and appreciation that helps partners stay emotionally connected, even during conflict

One of the places I often see attachment dynamics show up in my office is within these core elements.

Regarding commitment, one partner may want the relationship to move toward more closeness, clarity, or long-term security while the other feels hesitant or fearful. Resistance is often rooted in fear of vulnerability, loss of independence, or past relational pain. For some partners, closeness doesn't automatically feel safe. It can feel overwhelming, exposing, or even risky.

When you begin to understand behavior through an attachment lens, you stop seeing one partner as "too much" and the other as "not enough" and start seeing both as trying to feel safe in different ways.

EXAMPLE

Pam and Felix have been dating for four years. Pam wants to get married. Felix avoids the conversations, and when he feels forced to discuss it, he brings up his past relationships and fears around being financially impacted again, as he was in his divorce.

Pam and Felix can shift toward safety by Felix saying, "I notice I shut down when we talk about this. It's not because I don't care. I think I'm actually scared, and I want to work through that with you."

REMEMBER

Avoidance is often fear — fear of repeating past pain, losing autonomy, or being overwhelmed.

EXAMPLE

Val and Robert are married. Val found out that Robert had an affair earlier in their marriage, although it was years ago. Consequently, it has become difficult for Val to separate what is truth from Robert and what is not. Her anxious attachment has been activated and she is constantly scanning for safety. Is he telling the truth? Is he where he said he was going? Robert feels scrutinized and becomes defensive or withdrawn, which only reinforces Val's fear and uncertainty.

A shift toward safety might look like Robert saying, "I understand why it's hard for you to trust after what happened. I'm going to be transparent with you, even when it's uncomfortable."

And Val can respond, "I don't want to feel this anxious all the time. I know it affects you. I'm trying to feel safe again. Please be patient with me."

REMEMBER

Under trust, attachment injuries can become especially visible. When the relationship is not consistently prioritized or when there has been betrayal, such as in the case of affairs or secrecy, safety is deeply impacted. Partners begin to question whether they can rely on one another emotionally, not just behaviorally.

EXAMPLE

Gabriel and Mike have been dating for three years. Gabriel feels most connected when he and Mike are being intimate regularly and when Mike is attentive daily. Mike comes from a household where he had a lot of independence. Too much closeness feels smothering for Mike. When Gabriel asks for more connection, Mike shuts down.

A shift toward safety might look like Gabriel saying, "I think I've been coming on strong because I miss feeling close to you.

Mike may reply, "I want to be close to you too. It's not your fault, but too much closeness can be overwhelming for me. Can we start small?"

What's happening here is a difference in needs around closeness. One partner reaches for connection to feel safe, while the other requires a lot of space to feel safe. Without understanding this, both partners can begin to feel misunderstood.

Building Emotional Safety in Your Relationship

REMEMBER

Safety is built over time with consistency. You cannot have safety in a relationship without boundaries.

You can find a lot of information and misinformation about boundaries online. Sometimes the information frames boundaries as rigid walls or ultimatums. Others treat them as something you use only when someone has done something wrong.

In the context of attachment and emotional safety, boundaries are much more foundational than that. At their simplest, boundaries are limits that protect connection. They can be:

- Physical, such as space, proximity, or touch
- Emotional, such as honoring your own feelings and respecting the feelings of your partner

Understanding what boundaries have to do with attachment

When your attachment system is activated — when you feel insecure, disconnected, or unsure — you don't always respond in balanced ways. For example,

- People with anxious attachment may
  - Become overly accommodating and ignore their own limits
  - Overstep their partner's boundaries in an effort to feel close
  - Create rigid, reactive boundaries out of fear
- People who feel avoidant or overwhelmed may
  - Shut down
  - Create distance without explanation
  - Use boundaries as a way to disconnect rather than stay in relationship

In both cases, the goal is the same: to feel safe. However, the way it shows up can disrupt safety instead of supporting it.

REMEMBER

Creating boundaries as a foundation for safety

Healthy boundaries are not about pushing each other away or creating brick walls. They're what make it possible to stay connected without losing yourself or crossing someone else's space or limits.

REMEMBER

Healthy boundaries allow partners to feel the following kinds of things:

- I can be close to you and still be me.
- I can express my needs without fear.
- I can trust that I won't be invaded or overwhelmed.
- I can trust that you will be there for me.

TIP

Chapter 17 explores boundaries more deeply, especially how to balance independence and connection.

Creating a Couple Bubble

PACT stands for Psychobiological Approach to Couple Therapy. In PACT therapy, Stan Tatkin describes the idea of a couple bubble, a shared agreement between partners to protect one another and the relationship from harm.

At its core, the couple bubble is represents this idea: You and I are on the same team. We take care of each other.

This doesn't mean couples won't experience conflict or moments of disconnection. It means that even in those moments, the relationship itself is treated as something worth protecting.

REMEMBER

From an attachment perspective, partners are constantly asking questions like:

- Are you there for me?
- Do I matter to you?
- Will you respond when I reach for you?

TIP

When partners prioritize one another, keep each other in mind, and repair the relationship after conflict, they begin to create a reliable sense of emotional safety.

Safety, in this sense, is about knowing that when something goes wrong, your partner will move toward you, not away.

TIP

As the couple bubble strengthens, something shifts. Partners begin to feel things like:

- We're in this together.
- I don't have to handle everything on my own.
- Even when things get hard, you'll come back to me.

REMEMBER

When people are securely attached, there's a strong sense of reliability. Over time, this shared sense of "us" helps people get through the challenges of life.

REMEMBER

Attachment theory focuses on how people's early experiences with caregivers shape how they connect with others as adults. Tatkin's couple bubble shows how the couple bubble provides a safe space where adults feel secure. When adults have this sense of security, they can face life's stressors because they feel supported by their partner. This bubble also helps partners to coregulate by helping each other to soothe when they are distressed.

Restoring Safety (Repair)

One of my favorite relationship tools to reach couples is repair. It seems like a simple concept, but there is actually so much that most couples don't know about repairing.

REMEMBER

Most people think that repairing means just saying, "I'm sorry." Although apologies can be part of repair, they're only a small piece of it.

John Gottman defines repair as any step that you take that reduces negativity in the moment and helps shift the interaction toward connection. This means that repair can be:

- A softer tone
- Sharing your feelings

» Saying, "Wait, let me remind . . ."

» Sharing a hug, a touch, or warmth

From an attachment lens, repair is how you restore a sense of safety after it's been disrupted. For many couples, this can be unfamiliar territory because no one has taught them how to do this. They may have grown up in homes where conflict meant silence, escalation, or avoidance.

EXAMPLE

Zoë and Keith sit on the couch after dinner. Zoë has been trying to talk about feeling disconnected lately, but as the conversation starts to get more emotional, Keith goes quiet. He looks away. His body shifts. He starts to shut down. Zoë feels it immediately. Her chest tightens and her voice speeds up. She says, "This is what you always do. You just disappear on me." Keith feels the pull to withdraw even more, say nothing, and wait for it to pass.

But this time, he does something different. He takes a breath and says, "I can feel myself wanting to shut down right now." Zoë pauses. Keith continues, "I'm not trying to pull away from you. I think I'm just getting overwhelmed. I don't always know what to say in these moments."

The tone in the room changes. Zoë's shoulders drop. "Okay, that helps," she says more softly. "It just feels like you're leaving me."

"I'm not," Keith replies. "I'm here. I just need a second sometimes."

Instead of the conversation escalating, both Zoë and Keith feel heard and understood.

This is how repair creates safety.

Developing Emotional Attunement

When I think of an emotionally attuned couple, I think of a couple who really know each other.

They know what stresses their partner out before it's even said out loud. They can hear the tone shift in their voice and recognize that something deeper is happening. They understand each other's histories and the small signs that their partner is feeling off or not themselves.

This is the kind of knowing that creates emotional safety.

REMEMBER

From an attachment perspective, emotional attunement helps answer a core question that people carry into relationships: Are you there for me?

TIP

Sue Johnson describes this using the acronym ARE: accessibility, responsiveness, and engagement. In other words, can I reach you, can I rely on you to respond to me, and will you stay emotionally present with me?

John Gottman described what emotional attunement looks like in everyday life. Here are some examples:

- Noticing when your partner looks upset and asking, "Hey, what's going on?"
- Putting you phone down when your partner starts talking.
- Responding to your partner's attempts to connect (what Gottman calls bids for connection).

Attunement becomes even more important during conflict. Most couples don't fight because of a surface issue. Sue Johnson calls these vulnerable places "raw spots". They're old wounds around rejection, abandonment, or not feeling important. When those raw spots gets triggered, partners often react from a more protective place such as anger, criticism, withdrawal, or defensiveness.

REMEMBER

Emotional attunement can break this cycle because there is a different outcome when a partner can listen, validate, and be present instead of becoming reactive and protective.

EXAMPLE

Tyler and Luis have been dating for three years. Tyler would like to spend more time with Luis. Luis is juggling the demands of raising his children, managing his career, and handling other responsibilities, leaving him with very little free time. Although Luis cares deeply for Tyler and wants to build a life together, Tyler experiences the lack of time together as distance and disconnection.

During therapy Luis shares how overwhelmed and stretched thin he feels. As he talks, he begins to shut down and withdraw. Rather than criticizing him or demanding more time together, Tyler reaches over and says, "I know you're your carrying a lot right now, and I also miss you. I want us to figure this out together." When Tyler does this, Luis is able to stay present. This is emotional attunement.

TIP

To assess whether you're emotionally attuned to your partner, here are some questions you can reflect on:

- Do I notice when something is off with my partner?
- When my partner shares something emotional, do I try to understand it, fix it, defend it, or minimize it?
- Do I respond in a way that helps my partner feel seen and heard?
- When things get tense, can I stay present or do I shut down, get defensive, or check out?
- Does my partner experience me as someone they can reach, rely on, and feel connected to?

IN THIS CHAPTER

» Expressing your needs to others

» Navigating conflict and discovering techniques to work through issues

» Choosing to turn toward others

Chapter 16

Establishing a Culture of Communication

From an attachment perspective, communication isn't just about exchanging information. It's about answering a deeper question that sits underneath nearly every interaction. That question is, "Are you there for me?"

Our conversations and conflicts can strengthen or weaken our sense of emotional safety. In this chapter, I help you understand practical ways to communicate with greater clarity and connection. You find out how to express your needs and manage conflict, take healthy breaks during difficult conversations, repair disconnection, create emotional safety, and build the habit of turning toward the people who matter most.

Expressing Needs Clearly

One of the biggest challenges in relationships is that many people don't do well with expressing what they need, but they react when their needs aren't met. Here are some examples:

- Instead of saying, "I need more time with you," a person may say, "You're always working."

» Instead of saying, "I'm feeling a little disconnected," someone may announce, "You never pay attention to me."

Statements like these are is especially common when attachment is activated. When a person feels insecure, they often move into a protest state.

REMEMBER

Protest refers to actions that you take when your emotional connection to your partner feels threatened. If you have anxious attachment, protest can exhibit as a desperate feeling to make contact or taking actions to bring your partner closer. If you have avoidant attachment, protest can look like deactivating strategies, such as withdrawing or minimizing.

TIP

Clear communication starts with slowing down and asking yourself, *What do I actually need right now?*

Put your answer into simple, direct language: For example,

» I think I just need a little more connection tonight.

» I could really use some reassurance right now.

This kind of communication lowers defensiveness and makes it easier for your partner to respond.

Navigating Conflict

REMEMBER

Conflict is not always a sign that something is wrong in your relationship. In fact, many of the issues couples argue about are what John Gottman calls *perpetual problems* — problems that aren't solvable, such as differences in personality, opposing preferences, or needs that don't fully go away. Maybe you're highly social and your partner is more introverted, or you're a saver and they're a spender. You can each adjust these things, but at their core, the traits are unlikely to entirely change.

From an attachment perspective, conflict is often the moment when deeper fears get activated, such as fear of rejection, fear of overwhelm, or fear of being too much or not enough.

So while it may look like you're arguing about dishes, time, or tone, what's often underneath is something more vulnerable, such as:

» Do I matter to you?

» Are you going to show up for me?

» Am I safe with you?

TIP

When you start to see conflict this way, the goal shifts. Instead of trying to eliminate conflict, you begin learning how to stay connected *through* it.

Managing differences

One of the biggest myths in relationships is that compatibility means agreement. In reality, healthy couples learn how to stay emotionally connected even when they see things differently.

You have to have flexibility and curiosity to manage differences with your partner:

» Help me understand why this matters to you.

» I don't see it the same way, but I want to get where you're coming from.

TIP

When partners feel understood, they're far more open to compromise. When they feel dismissed or judged, they tend to dig in.

One of the ways that I work on this with couples is by helping them maintain connection in the presence of difference.

EXAMPLE

Carmela and Tristen came to couples therapy to work on navigating conflict. Their relationship was feeling more and more disconnected due to their differences. Carmela and Tristen were engaged to be married, and they were planning on building a family together. They both had busy, fulfilling careers. It became evident in therapy that Carmela had an active social life. She required time to process with her friends. This felt deeply important to her. Tristen, on the other hand, didn't have this need. She had a few good friends whom she saw every couple of months. This insight into their differences helped Tristen to understand Carmela's needs, which enabled her to stop experiencing Carmela's time with her friends as abandonment. At the same time, Carmela listened and began to understand Tristen's perspective. Together, they figure out how to find win-win situations.

Taking time-outs (without disconnecting)

There are moments in conflict when your body is simply too activated to have a productive conversation. For example, if you notice your heart rate rising, your speech getting faster, your thoughts narrowing, or a sudden urge to shut down or push back, you're probably too activated. The walls go up. Defensiveness or criticism takes over.

REMEMBER

This is what John Gottman calls emotional flooding, and what Sue Johnson describes as attachment panic. Read more in Chapter 11.

When you get in this situation, continuing the conversation usually makes things worse rather than better. You're no longer responding to your partner. You're reacting from a dysregulated nervous system. This is where a time-out becomes essential.

Unfortunately, there's something most couples get wrong. A time-out isn't the same as walking away, shutting down, or avoiding the issue. A healthy time-out is a form of regulation, not disconnection. When you do a time-out correctly, it can be a way to protect your relationship.

It's a way of saying, "I want to stay in this with you, but I need to calm my body so I can show up better."

TIP

A good timeout has three parts:

- **You name what's happening:** "I'm getting overwhelmed."
- **You reassure the connection:** "I care about this and I want to come back to it."
- **You give a clear plan to return:** "Can we take 20 minutes and come back?"

Without these three pieces, a time-out can feel like abandonment, especially to a partner who already fears disconnection. When handled well, though, time-outs can be incredibly healing. They teach both partners that conflict doesn't have to spiral, and that taking space doesn't mean losing the relationship.

EXAMPLE

Sasha and Clarence are in the middle of an argument about household responsibilities. Sasha feels overwhelmed and unsupported. Clarence feels like nothing he does is ever enough.

As the conversation escalates, Sasha's voice gets sharper and faster. Clarence starts to shut down, crossing his arms and looking away. Clarence suddenly says, "I'm done with this," and walks out of the room.

Sasha is left standing there, flooded and alone. Her anxiety spikes even higher. In her mind, this confirms her fear: *He doesn't care. He's leaving me.*

Clarence, meanwhile, tells himself he just needed space, and he doesn't realize that his exit felt like rejection.

I want to examine another way this could have played out. Sarah and Clarence are at the same moment, but this time, Clarence handles it differently.

EXAMPLE

Clarence pauses and says, "I'm getting really overwhelmed right now. I don't want to shut down or say something I regret. Can we take 20 minutes to calm down and then come back to this?"

Sasha is still activated, but something shifts. Instead of feeling abandoned, she feels reassured. She knows he's not leaving the relationship and that he's trying to step away to calm down.

Clarence steps away, takes time to regulate, and returns when he's calmer. When they resume, the conversation is slower, more grounded, and far more productive.

REMEMBER

The difference is in how the break is communicated.

Developing a code word or safe signal

TIP

When conflict escalates quickly, it can be hard to pause in a calm, thoughtful way. It can be hard for some people to find the words when they are overwhelmed. This is where a shared signal can help.

Some couples create a simple code word or phrase that means, "We're getting off track. Let's pause."

The word or phrase might be something light or even slightly humorous, but the meaning is serious. The goal is to protect the connection while emotions are running high.

EXAMPLE

Julian and Morgan are dating. Julian feels best in a clean, organized environment. Clutter prevents him from relaxing. Morgan is more relaxed with messes, and she doesn't prioritize keeping their space tidy. One day Morgan comes home from work and leaves her shoes in middle of the living room, her purse on the counter, and her sweater on the chair. She even leaves her books, coffee, and keys on the coffee table.

Julian sees Morgan's mess, and he is activated. He thinks, *She knows I just cleaned up, and she knows how much this stresses me out, but she does it anyway because she just doesn't care about me.* Julian makes a critical comment. When these scenarios occur, Morgan typically feels judged and controlled, and she shuts down. She usually leaves the room and puts on headphones. Morgan's attachment style is avoidant. When Morgan leaves, it usually triggers Julian's anxious attachment. Since they have been in therapy, they developed a code word to indicate that they need a break. Their code word is *watermelon*.

One evening, Julian notices the clutter and feels himself becoming flooded. Instead of criticizing Morgan, he says "watermelon." Morgan recognizes that he's becoming overwhelmed and responds, "OK, let's take a break." They spend 30 minutes apart. Julian takes a walk, and Morgan works on a project. When they return to the conversation, Julian says, "I've realized the mess makes me feel anxious and out of control." Rather than accusing Morgan of not caring. Morgan is able to hear him without becoming defensive, and they come up with a plan to work together on this in a way that considers both of their feelings.

Returning to each other

In the world of attachment, a conflict isn't just a disagreement; it's a rupture. Repairing that rupture is essential. Your partner isn't the enemy. The negative cycle is.

TIP

For repairing a rupture, Dr. Sue Johnson emphasizes the importance of recognizing the negative cycle or the spin. Instead of pointing a finger or criticizing, the focus is on the we. "We're stuck in this loop where I push and you pull."

Dr. John Gottman's research found that healthy couples repair quickly and regularly rather than avoiding a repair altogether or waiting a long time to repair.

A repair can take the form of:

- Sharing your feelings
- Rewinding
- Softening your approach
- Taking responsibility
- Taking a time-out

TIP

Some things that you may say as part of a repair include:

- "Hey, I've been thinking about earlier. I don't like how that went."
- "I think I got defensive. I want to try again."
- "I miss you. Can we reset?"

REMEMBER

These moments of reconnection build trust over time. They send a powerful message: Even when we struggle, we can find our way back.

Viewing conflict as connection

Conflict isn't necessarily a sign that something is wrong in a relationship. Research consistently shows that healthy couples are not conflict-free couples. Rather, they are couples who have learned how to use conflict as an opportunity for connection. They're couples who have learned how to disagree while maintaining respect and connection.

Attachment researchers have found that many relationship conflicts are driven by deeper needs for connection, reassurance, and emotional safety. Beneath disagreements about daily issues are often saying such things as:

- "Do I matter to you?"
- "Can I count on you when I need you?"
- "This matters to me."
- "I need something here."
- "I don't want to feel this distance between us."

In other words, conflict is often less about the topic being discussed and more about the need that the topic represents.

REMEMBER

When you understand the need beneath the argument, it becomes easier to respond to your partner instead of simply reacting to the disagreement.

Turning toward Instead of Away

At the heart of a strong communication culture are small, everyday moments. John Gottman describes these moments as *bids for connection* or ways partners move toward each other through a comment, a question, a glance, or a small gesture.

In each of these moments, you have a choice:

- Turn toward by responding and engaging
- Turn away by ignoring or missing the bid
- Turn against by responding with irritation or dismissal

Turning toward doesn't have to be big or demonstrative. It can be as simple as saying:

- "Tell me more."
- "Yeah, I see that."
- "Come here."

REMEMBER

Over time, these small responses build a sense of emotional safety by communicating:

- "I see you."
- "I care."
- "I'm here."

TIP

In attachment terms, turning toward is how partners stay emotionally accessible, responsive and engaged in everyday life, not just during conflict. These small moments of connection become the foundation that help couples stay connected when things get harder.

5

Putting the Tools into Practice

IN THIS PART . . .

Acquire practical tools to use when navigating conflict, feeling triggered, or trying to build stronger emotional connection.

Find out about working with a therapist to change attachment styles.

Work to identify attachment triggers and manage them.

Discover how attachment styles shape dating relationships and approach dating with greater self-awareness.

IN THIS CHAPTER

» Improving communication for understanding

» Discovering tools for expressing feelings

» Creating healthy habits, boundaries, and rituals that strengthen connection

Chapter 17 Exploring Tools for Couples

When couples first fall in love, connection often feels easy. Conversations flow, misunderstandings are quickly repaired, and affection comes naturally. Over time, stress, responsibilities, and old attachment wounds or patterns can make communication harder.

When couples don't have the tools to navigate those challenging moments, small misunderstandings can turn into recurring conflicts. Healthy relationships are built on skills that facilitate communication. The tools in this chapter are some of the most important skills couples can learn to strengthen communication, reduce conflict, and deepen connection. They're like tools in a toolbox. The more tools you have, the more options you have when challenges arise.

Crossing the Divide: The Importance of Communication

Many couples say their main problem is communication. In my experience, when couples say this, they're usually having trouble navigating conflict or understanding each other emotionally.

REMEMBER

Communication isn't just about exchanging information. It's about helping your partner understand your internal world and making space to understand theirs. When communication breaks down, couples can feel like they're standing on opposite sides of a divide. This is particularly true when an attachment wound is activated.

One partner's feeling may be, "You don't understand me." At the same time, the other partner may feel, "Nothing I say ever seems good enough."

EXAMPLE

Emma and Roman have been dating for three years. Roman has a daughter and shares custody with his ex. At times, he doesn't fully loop Emma into what's happening in that part of his life. Plans change and decisions are made, and Emma finds out after the fact. When this happens, Emma feels anxious. To her, it feels like distance. She starts to wonder, *Why didn't he tell me? Did I do something wrong? Is he pulling away?* So she asks questions, trying to understand what's going on and reconnect. From Emma's perspective, she's protecting the relationship. From Roman's perspective, those questions feel like pressure. When he feels pressured, he shuts down. "I don't know what you want me to say," he might respond, or he goes quiet altogether.

As a result, the cycle escalates. Emma experiences silence as rejection or abandonment, so she pushes a little harder for clarity. Roman experiences her questions as criticism or a judgment that he's somehow failing, so he withdraws even more. Both partners feel misunderstood.

Emma thinks, You don't understand me. Roman thinks, Nothing I do is good enough.

Researchers call this form of attachment where one partner reaches for connection while the other pulls away to reduce stress a *pursue-withdraw* cycle. Without communication tools, couples can quickly fall into patterns of defensiveness, criticism, and withdrawal. The goal of the tools in this chapter is to help couples cross that divide, so partners can move from reacting to each other to understanding on another.

Relationship researcher Dr. John Gottman described four common communication patterns that show up in distressed relationships. He called them the four horsemen: criticism, defensiveness, contempt, and stonewalling. You don't need to memorize these terms. What matters is recognizing the pattern you and your partner fall into when things start to feel tense or disconnected.

REMEMBER

From an attachment perspective, these reactions aren't random; they're protective. They show up when something in the relationship begins to feel unsafe, uncertain, or emotionally out of reach.

The four reactions often show up when people are experiencing big feelings:

» **Criticism** often comes from a place of protest: "Do I matter to you?"

» **Defensiveness** can be a response to shame or feeling blamed.

» **Contempt** often signals deeper hurt that hasn't been repaired.

» **Stonewalling** or withdrawal is often the nervous system trying to regulate overwhelm.

Sharing your feelings

Chapter 12 covers why labeling emotions is important. Once you've identified the emotions you're feeling, you need to share them with your partner. Sharing feelings is one of the most powerful ways couples build connection.

When partners talk openly about their emotional experiences, they give each other access to what's happening beneath the surface. Yet for many people, sharing feelings is surprisingly difficult. One of the biggest reasons is fear of vulnerability.

When you share a feeling with your partner, you're revealing something personal and emotionally exposed. In that moment, you trust that your partner will respond with care rather than criticism, dismissal, or indifference. For people who have been hurt in past relationships or who grew up in families where emotions were not openly discussed, sharing can feel risky. Instead of saying what they truly feel, many people protect themselves by speaking indirectly. They may express frustration, criticism, or problem-solving instead of the emotion underneath.

For example, someone might say, "You never spend time with me anymore." But the feeling underneath the complaint might actually be, "I miss you."

Another reason sharing feelings can be difficult is that many people were never taught the language of emotions. In some families, emotions were rarely discussed. As a child, a person may have learned to focus on behavior, responsibility, or problem-solving rather than identifying what they were feeling internally. In adulthood, that same person may struggle to find the words to describe their emotional experiences.

A third reason people hesitate to share feelings is the fear that it will start a conflict rather than create connection. They may think, "If I say I'm hurt, we'll just end up arguing." To avoid that possibility, they stay silent. Unfortunately, unspoken feelings often build over time and eventually emerge as frustration, criticism, or distance.

From an attachment perspective, emotions are signals about the need for connection and safety in relationships. When partners hide those feelings, the real message gets lost. The challenge for many couples is learning to move from protective reactions to honest emotional sharing.

When partners are able to say things like:

» "I felt hurt when that happened."

» "I was scared we were drifting apart."

» "I felt lonely tonight."

they give their partner a clearer understanding of what is happening emotionally beneath the surface. This creates opportunities for empathy, comfort, and connection rather than misunderstanding and conflict.

REMEMBER

When you share your emotions, you're inviting your partner into your emotional world, which increases connection.

Using "I" statements

TIP

"I" statements are one of the simplest and most effective communication tools couples can use. Instead of accusing your partner, using an "I" statement focuses on your personal experience, what you feel, or what you need.

You might be wondering what this has to do with attachment. When your attachment system is activated, your brain is scanning for threat: Am I safe? Do I matter? Am I being rejected? In those moments, it's easy to move into criticism or defensiveness as a way to protect yourself. "I" statements can help interrupt that pattern. They allow you to express the underlying attachment need like wanting reassurance, closeness, or understanding without triggering your partner's defenses. Instead of escalating the cycle, you're inviting connection.

Instead of saying, "You never tell me what's going on," you can instead say, "I feel anxious when I don't know what's going on. I think I'm needing more connection or reassurance."

The first statement invites defensiveness. The second invites understanding.

TIP

A helpful formula for making an "I" statement is:

I feel . . .

when . . .

because . . .

EXAMPLE

For instance, "I feel hurt when plans change at the last minute because it makes me feel unimportant."

Or "I feel anxious when we avoid talking about money because it leaves me unsure about our future."

REMEMBER

"I" statements help partners express their emotions clearly while reducing blame.

Softening your startup

Research from Dr. Gottman suggests that the way a conversation begins often determines how it will end. If a conversation begins with criticism, blame, or sarcasm, the other partner is more likely to respond defensively. Consequently, the first few sentences of a difficult conversation make a difference in how the rest of the conversation will go.

A harsh startup might be something like, "You're always on your phone. You clearly don't care about this relationship."

A softer startup might be, "Can we talk about something that's been bothering me? I've been feeling a little disconnected lately."

TIP

Soft startups increase the chances that the conversation will stay calm and productive.

REMEMBER

From an attachment perspective, a softened startup isn't just a communication technique; it's an attachment move. When a person's attachment system is activated, their brain is scanning for signs of rejection, criticism, or disconnection. A softened startup reduces the likelihood that your partner's attachment system will become activated and defensive. Instead of leading with blame or criticism, it invites connections through vulnerability, helping both partners to feel safe and stay engaged.

Becoming Responsive

Demonstrating responsiveness means showing your partner that their emotions matter. Even when you disagree with the details of what your partner is saying, you can still respond to the emotion behind it.

You may say something such as, "I can see why that would upset you," or "That sounds like it was really stressful."

REMEMBER

Feeling responded to is one of the strongest predictors of relationship satisfaction. When partners feel ignored or dismissed, emotional distance grows. When partners feel acknowledged, connection grows.

In this section, I share some effective tools for being responsive while communicating with your partner.

Summarizing

One powerful listening skill is summarizing. Summarizing means briefly reflecting back what you heard your partner say. Summarizing is a way you can show your partner that you see them, you get them, and that they're not alone.

Here are some examples of summarizing what your partner has said:

- "So what I'm hearing is that you felt embarrassed when that happened."
- "It sounds like you've been feeling overwhelmed lately."

This simple step does two important things. First, it helps confirm whether you understood your partner correctly. Second, it communicates that you're genuinely trying to listen.

REMEMBER

Many arguments escalate simply because partners react before they have fully understood each other.

Validating each other

Validation is often misunderstood. Validating your partner does not mean agreeing with them. It simply means acknowledging that their feelings make sense from their perspective.

When your partner is upset and their attachment system is activated, it's helpful to confirm that their experience makes sense. This may mean saying something like, "I can understand why that situation felt frustrating," or "That would probably upset me too."

REMEMBER

When someone feel validated, their nervous system settles, and their defensiveness drops. Validation helps partners feel less alone in their emotional experience. When validated, partners feel safer.

In my office, I often see one partner trying to correct the other by saying, "I didn't ignore you. You're making a bid deal out of nothing."

And I'll say, "Can you help your partner feel understood before you explain your side?"

When they shift their approach to validation by saying something along these lines,

> "I can see how that felt like I was ignoring you. I get why that hurt,"

everything changes.

Responding with presence

At the core of attachment is the need to feel seen, safe, and emotionally connected to the people you love. One of the primary ways this happens is through emotional attunement — the experience of feeling that your partner is with you, not just physically but also emotionally.

Researchers like Dr. Gottman have studied what this looks like in everyday moments. He describes it as turning toward your partner and responding with presence. (Chapter 16 talks about partners turning toward each other.)

TIP

Presence isn't about fixing. It's about being with your partner in their experience.

Offering presence involves:

- Putting down your phone
- Making eye contact
- Listening without interrupting
- Responding with curiosity

REMEMBER

Sometimes partners don't need advice or solutions. They want to feel heard.

I often see couples come to me with a focus on solving problems, working out logistics, making decisions, and getting clarity. But what they need first isn't an immediate solution. They need to sit with each other's experience. This is what strengthens the attachment bond. From that bond comes a deeper sense of safety.

REMEMBER

Being emotionally present communicates a powerful message:

- You matter to me.
- Your feelings matter to me.
- I'm here with you.

Checking In

Healthy couples don't talk only when there is a problem. They also check in regularly about how things are going. I regularly encourage couples to have weekly check-ins. This gives them an opportunity to ask one another, "How are you? How are we doing? What do we need more of? What do we need less of?"

I find that couples do best when they set aside the same time each week for a check-in. If they're not intentional about checking in, it's easy for these conversations to get pushed aside by busy schedules, work demands, parenting responsibilities, or other facets of everyday life.

REMEMBER

Regular check-ins help prevent resentment from building over time. Think of it as routine maintenance for your relationship.

Dr. Gottman calls this check-in the state of the union meeting. During this meeting couples can:

- Appreciate one another
- Discuss concerns
- Talk about upcoming plans
- Address small frustrations before they grow

REMEMBER

The goal of the check-in isn't to criticize each other but to stay connected and collaborative:

EXAMPLE

Brett and Marissa have been together for four years. They recently moved from Las Vegas, Nevada to California, and on the surface, their relationship showed clear signs of commitment and dedication. However, Marissa often felt shut out when she tried to connect on a deeper level. When she asked Brett about his work, his day, or his internal world, he tended to shut down or keep things vague.

In therapy, it became clear that Brett leaned toward an avoidant attachment style. Conversations involving emotions felt uncomfortable and exposing for him, so he coped by staying on the surface or withdrawing altogether. To support their growth, I encouraged them to begin a weekly state of the union meeting.

This structure created a predictable and contained space for connection. For Brett, knowing there was a clear beginning, middle, and end to these conversations helped reduce his anxiety. It made emotional engagement feel more manageable and less overwhelming. For Marissa, the meetings provided a consistent opportunity she could rely on to feel heard and prioritized. Over time, we discussed how these conversations could become more organic. But in the early stages of attachment work, the structure itself became a form of safety, helping both partners move toward each other in a way that felt sustainable.

Creating Daily, Weekly, and Monthly Rituals

Rituals are small habits that strengthen connection. They help couples stay emotionally close even during busy seasons of life.

Daily rituals may include:

- Saying goodbye in the morning
- Texting during the day
- Checking in before bed

Weekly rituals could be:

- Having date night
- Doing a shared activity
- Taking a walk together

Examples of monthly rituals include:

- Reviewing goals
- Planning something fun
- Celebrating milestones

REMEMBER

These rituals create predictable opportunities for connection. When partners regularly connect, their nervous systems begin to register the relationship as a safe place. Without connection, misunderstandings can feel bigger, triggering patterns of pursuit, withdrawal, or shut down.

Having Boundaries

In general, healthy relationships require boundaries. Boundaries protect emotional safety and help partners treat each other with respect. In a secure relationship, both partners can stay emotionally connected and have limits.

Examples of relationship boundaries include:

- Avoiding insults during arguments
- Respecting personal space when needed
- Agreeing not to discuss sensitive topics when emotions are too high

REMEMBER

Boundaries are not about controlling your partner. They're about protecting the health of the relationship.

When relationships lack boundaries, there can be deterioration in the relationship:

- Resentment can build.
- One partner may overfunction.
- The other may underfunction.
- The relationship may become unstable.

In relationships where attachment wounds are activated, boundaries often get pulled to extremes. One partner may struggle to set any boundaries, while the other may become rigid or overly guarded:

- A person with anxious attachment may let boundaries collapse when connection feels threatened. As a result, they may
  - Override their own limits
  - Say yes when they mean no
  - Focus all their efforts on keeping the relationship intact
- A person with avoidant attachment may be too rigid with boundaries, and when connection feels overwhelming, they may
  - Create distance
  - Set hard or abrupt limits

TIP

Secure boundaries sit in the middle. They allow you to stay connected to your partner while also staying connected to yourself. Porous boundaries are boundaries that are overly permeable, such as a garden with no fence, where anyone can enter. Rigid boundaries are on the other end of the continuum, such as a garden with a brick wall around it.

Creating an I–You–We

Strong relationships balance three identities:

- I, which is your individual self
- You, which is your partner's individual self
- We, which is the relationship you build together

Problems can arise when one of these identities becomes too dominant. If everything becomes "we," partners may lose their sense of independence. If everything becomes "I," partners may drift apart emotionally.

REMEMBER

Healthy couples protect all three.

EXAMPLE

Nayeli and Zane had been together since high school. They had a long history. Nayeli stayed at Zane's apartment most of the time. They were dog parents together, and they spent every day together. Zane wanted to meet up periodically with his buddies for gaming or to play darts. Whenever this happened, there would be conflict. Zane felt smothered by Nayeli's reactions and expectations. In therapy, I highlighted that healthy couples have an I, a you, and a we. I educated the couple on the importance of Zane having his own hobbies and space, and Nayeli also having her own hobbies, friends, and space while together they also protected the we.

Comparing Dependence and Interdependence

Healthy relationships are built on interdependence. *Dependence* means one partner relies entirely on the other. *Independence* means partners operate separately. *Interdependence* means partners support each other while still maintaining their own identity. In an interdependent relationship, partners can say, "I am capable on my own, but life is better when we support each other."

People are wired to need connection. Wanting support, closeness, and reassurance from a partner isn't weakness. It's part of being human. At the same time, relying completely on your partner for your sense of stability or identity can create pressure and imbalance in the relationship.

This is where interdependence comes in. When you're in an interdependent relationship, you can stand on your own and lean on your partner without losing yourself in the process.

REMEMBER

Interdependence is the balance between connection and individuality.

This kind of balance creates a more secure attachment where both partners feel connected but not trapped — supported but not responsible for each other's entire emotional world.

IN THIS CHAPTER

- **Understanding what therapy is**
- **Exploring how therapy brings change**
- **Taking a look at individual therapy, couples therapy, and couples intensives**

Chapter 18

Working with a Therapist

If you've made it this far, you've likely started to see how you respond in relationships, what triggers you, and how your attachment style shows up in everyday life. And while insight is important, insight alone doesn't always create change.

Therapy can also help. It offers something that's hard to create on your own: a space where you can slow things down, understand yourself more deeply, learn new skills, and begin to respond differently.

For many people, the idea of therapy brings up mixed feelings. You might have the following questions:

- Do I really need therapy?
- What would I even talk about?
- How is this going to be useful?
- What if it doesn't help?

These questions are normal.

Working with a therapist means you're choosing to better understand yourself and how you connect with others. From an attachment perspective, therapy is more than just talking about problems. It's about experiencing something different.

In a healthy therapeutic relationship, you begin to feel seen, understood, and responded to.

Over time, this can help reshape how you relate, not just in therapy, but in your everyday relationships. Change happens not just through insight but through new emotional experiences. Therapy becomes a place where those experiences can begin.

This chapter looks at what psychotherapy is, what different types of therapy are and how they can support your growth.

Looking at Psychotherapy

When people hear the word *psychotherapy*, they often imagine sitting (or lying) on a couch talking about their childhood. And while your past can absolutely be part of the work, therapy is usually much more practical and present-focused than people expect.

The focus of therapy depends on your needs:

- Understanding patterns in your relationships
- Managing anxiety, stress, or overwhelming emotions
- Developing new skills
- Working through past experiences that still impact you
- Doing inner child work
- Improving communication and connection

TIP

In terms of attachment, therapy helps you begin to notice *how* you respond when you feel insecure, overwhelmed, or disconnected and gives you tools to respond differently.

For example, when you're working in therapy on your attachment style, you may start to notice:

- How quickly your body reacts in certain situations
- How your thoughts shift when you feel triggered
- How your behavior follows those internal reactions

A therapist helps you slow these moments down so you can begin to understand them rather than react automatically. Over time, this understanding creates more choice for you. Instead of feeling stuck in the same patterns, you begin to:

- Pause before reacting
- Communicate more clearly
- Respond in ways that feel more aligned with who you want to be

It's about becoming more aware, more intentional, and more connected to yourself and to others.

Understanding How Therapy Leads to Change

Neuroplasticity refers to the brain's ability to change and adapt over time. Rather than being fixed and unchanging, your brain is constantly forming new connections based on what you practice and experience.

This adaptability is one of the reasons therapy can be so effective.

REMEMBER

Each time you respond differently to a situation, you strengthen new pathways in your brain. In relationships, this may look like figuring out how to stay present during conflict, soften your approach, or respond to your partner in a way that builds connection rather than distance.

At first, adjusting your responses can feel unnatural. You may understand what to do but still fall back into old patterns. That doesn't mean therapy isn't working. It means your brain is still learning. Over time, with repetition, the new responses begin to feel more automatic, and the effort to respond in the new ways will be less difficult.

Examining Common Therapy Approaches

There are many different therapy approaches that can help people better understand themselves, their relationships, and their attachment patterns. In this section, you discover some of the most common approaches and how they can support healing and healthier relationships.

Individual therapy

Individual therapy focuses on you, your thoughts, emotions, patterns, and experiences. In therapy, you have a space to better understand why you respond the way you do and begin shifting patterns that aren't working.

In individual therapy, you might explore things like:

- How your past experiences shape your current reactions
- What beliefs you hold about yourself, others, and relationships
- How you cope with stress, anxiety, or difficult emotions

REMEMBER

Over time, therapy helps you become more aware of your internal world. You may start to notice your emotions sooner, understand your triggers more clearly, and feel more intentional in how you respond.

Different therapy models or approaches are simply different ways of understanding what's happening inside of you and how change happens. Some common approaches you might come across are cognitive behavioral therapy (CBT), Internal Family Systems (IFS), and Emotionally Focused Therapy (EFT):

- **CBT** focuses on identifying and changing unhelpful thought patterns and behaviors. When attachment gets activated, a person's brain often can catastrophize with thoughts like, "They're pulling away," or "I'm not important." CBT helps you identify those automatic thoughts, question their accuracy, and replace them with more balanced interpretations.

  TIP

  CBT helps attachment healing by helping you change the internal narrative that fuels insecurity so you can show up in relationships with more stability.

- **IFS** is based on the idea that each person has different parts of themselves. For example, one part of you might want closeness, while another part pulls away to protect you. In therapy, you learn to understand these parts instead of fighting them so you can respond to yourself with more clarity and compassion. Sometimes people refer to this as inner child work.

  TIP

  In IFS, the behaviors that are labeled as anxious or avoidant aren't flaws. They're parts of you that developed to protect something more vulnerable.

- **EFIT** is the individual version of /emotionally focused therapy, an attachment-based approach often used with couples. It focuses on emotions and connection, especially in relationships. It helps you understand what's happening underneath your reactions and how that shows up in the way you relate to others.

REMEMBER

Even if your therapist doesn't name a specific model, they may be drawing from one of these ways of thinking. Many therapists pull from more than one model depending on what you need.

Body-based therapy

Not all therapy happens through talking alone. Sometimes, your body holds on to experiences in ways that your mind can't easily explain. You might feel tension, anxiety, or a sense of shutdown without fully understanding why. Body-based therapies focus on helping you tune in to those physical experiences and work through them. These approaches recognize that healing isn't just cognitive; it's also physical and emotional.

For example, EMDR (eye movement desensitization reuptake) and brainspotting are two modalities that work with how the brain and body store emotional experiences. By focusing on specific eye positions and body sensations, people can process and release distress that may feel stuck.

Body-based therapy can be especially helpful if:

- You feel overwhelmed or shut down quickly.
- You feel triggered and you don't know why.
- You struggle to put your experiences into words.
- You notice strong physical reactions to stress or triggers.

TIP

Rather than trying to "think your way out" of distress, these approaches help your nervous system settle so you can process experiences more fully.

Couples therapy

Couples therapy focuses on the dynamic between you and your partner and what happens between you. I often tell clients in couples therapy that they aren't my clients; their relationship is my client.

Couples therapy also helps uncover the attachment needs, fears, and protective strategies that drive many relationship conflicts. Often, the surface reason for an argument is less important than the deeper need for connection, reassurance, safety, or autonomy underneath it.

Couples therapy examines the patterns two people get stuck in together, especially during conflict, disconnection, or stress.

When you're working with your partner in couples therapy, you may begin to notice such things as:

- How small moments escalate into larger conflicts
- When you engage in patterns like criticism, defensiveness, or shutting down
- How each partner's needs and fears show up in the relationship

A big part of couples therapy is figuring out how to respond differently in those moments. You may discover how to soften how you bring something up, stay present instead of shutting down, or repair after conflict.

TIP

Couples therapy also gives individuals greater clarity about what the other person in the relationship is feeling. It helps partners better understand each other's internal experiences and what's underneath the reactions. Often, what looks like anger, withdrawal, or criticism is connected to deeper needs like wanting to feel valued, secure, or understood.

Over time, couples begin to shift from reacting against each other to working together. With practice, new patterns begin to replace old ones, creating a stronger sense of connection and emotional safety.

Types of couples therapy

There are different approaches to couples therapy, but most focus on helping you understand your patterns and build a stronger sense of connection. Here are two widely used approaches:

- **Gottman Method:** This approach focuses on strengthening communication, managing conflict, and building trust. The therapist may work with you on tools for handling disagreements, expressing needs more clearly, and strengthening your day-to-day connection.
- **Emotionally Focused Therapy (EFT):** EFT focuses on emotions and attachment. It helps you understand the deeper feelings and needs underneath conflict, such as the desire to feel secure, valued, and connected. If you read about EFIT earlier in this chapter, EFT is the couple's version of the same attachment-based approach.

REMEMBER

While these approaches may look different, they share a similar goal: helping you move out of reactive patterns and into more secure, connected interactions.

Couples therapy intensives

Some couples choose to go beyond weekly sessions by participating in therapy intensives. An intensive is a longer, more focused format that's often held over one or two days. The longer period gives partners extended time working through patterns, understanding the relationship, and practicing with new tools.

This format can be helpful if:

- You feel stuck in the same patterns.
- You want to make progress more quickly.
- Scheduling weekly sessions feels difficult.

TIP

Intensives allow you to go deeper without the stop-and-start rhythm of weekly therapy.

IN THIS CHAPTER

» **Understanding your triggers if you're avoidant**

» **Recognizing your triggers if you're anxious**

Chapter 19
Knowing Your Triggers

During moments in relationships, your reaction may feel bigger than the situation in front of you. Maybe your partner doesn't respond to a text, which suddenly sets your mind racing. Or they come home distracted, and you feel a wave of irritation or distance before you even understand why.

This is what it means to get *triggered*.

When attachment gets activated, your nervous system moves quickly to protect you. Your brain scans for danger. *Am I about to be rejected? Controlled? Ignored?* These reactions are shaped by your past experiences and the ways you learned to stay safe in relationships.

Some people respond to being triggered by moving closer, seeking reassurance, or trying to get a response. For others, it looks like pulling back, shutting down, or creating distance (or a combination of those things).

REMEMBER

The reactions are attempts to protect something vulnerable underneath.

This chapter explains how attachment triggers show up differently depending on your attachment style. It explores what happens when avoidant partners feel smothered or pressured and how to identify the emotions underneath the urge to withdraw or shut down. It also uncovers what happens when anxious partners feel insecure, rejected, or disconnected, including how to express those feelings rather than suppress them. Along the way, you find strategies for tolerating uncertainty, regulating your reactions, and respecting your partner's need for closeness or space while staying connected to your own needs.

Feeling Smothered or Pressured

If you tend to lean more avoidant, moments of closeness or emotional intensity can feel overwhelming. Someone observing an avoidant person might not be able to tell that they feel overwhelmed from the outside, but internally the avoidant person's system is saying, *This is too much. I need space.*

In these situations, you might notice yourself:

- Shutting down or going quiet.
- Feeling irritated or critical.
- Wanting to leave the conversation.
- Thinking, *I can't do this right now.*

In this section, I talk about the skills of labeling emotions, pausing and expressing your feelings rather than suppressing them.

Remembering to label emotions

One of the biggest challenges for avoidant partners is that the reaction often comes *before* their awareness kicks in. When you feel irritated or want to shut down, try to slow down enough to ask yourself these questions:

- What am I actually feeling right now?
- Is there stress, pressure, fear, or overwhelm underneath this urge I feel?

Giving what you're feeling a simple label like *I feel overwhelmed* or, *I feel pressure right now* can create just enough space for you to stay engaged instead of disappearing.

Pausing before shutting down

The instinct to withdraw is fast, and it works in the short term. It lowers the intensity you feel in a situation. But over time, your withdrawal leaves your partner feeling alone, and your retreat can deepen the cycle between you.

The goal isn't to force yourself to stay in a conversation when you're overwhelmed. Instead, you want to try to pause with intention instead of disappearing.

You can explain to your partner what you're doing by saying something like this:

- "I'm getting overwhelmed. I need a few minutes, but I'll come back."
- "I want to talk about this; I just need to settle first."

TIP

This small shift in how you react makes a big difference. You're still taking space for yourself, but you're doing it in a way that protects the relationship.

Expressing rather than suppressing

Avoidant patterns often involve pushing feelings down or minimizing them. However, suppressed emotions don't disappear. They still exist under the surface, and they tend to come out as distance, irritation, or disconnection.

When you're suppressing a feeling, you're usually trying to do one (or some) of the following things:

- Avoid conflict
- Prevent overwhelm
- Keep control of your emotions
- Protect yourself from feeling exposed or vulnerable

REMEMBER

In the moment, shutting down can feel like relief from immediate discomfort, but later, it can create significant disconnection.

Instead of holding everything in, practice expressing yourself. Here are some examples of things you can say:

- "This is hard for me to talk about."
- "I'm not sure what I'm feeling yet, but I don't want to shut down."
- I'm having some feelings.

TIP

Expressing yourself doesn't have to mean diving into a long emotional conversation. Communicating can be a challenge if you've been accustomed to shutting down rather than expressing yourself. It's important for partners to remember that someone with avoidant attachment need to pace themselves. You'll figure out how to regulate yourself and express more over time. Initially, the goal is to move toward your partner in small, manageable ways.

EXAMPLE

Sandra asks Ezequiel what's wrong. Ezequiel says, "Nothing," despite the fact that he feels irritated and worried. He withdraws, gets quiet, and later avoids Sandra for the rest of the evening.

When Ezequiel begins to express himself instead of suppressing what he's feeling, the scenario may play out like this: Sandra asks Ezequiel what's wrong, and Ezequiel replies, "I'm feeling a little overwhelmed. I don't think I can get into it fully, but I don't want you to feel shut out. Can we circle back to it?"

Feeling Insecure or Rejected

If you tend to lean more anxious, moments of distance or uncertainty can feel intense and urgent. Your system is scanning for signs of disconnection. *Are they pulling away? Did I do something wrong? Are they losing interest?*

You might notice:

- Wanting immediate reassurance
- Overthinking or replaying interactions
- Reaching out repeatedly
- Feeling a strong urge to "fix it" right away

REMEMBER

These reactions come from the need to feel secure, connected, and chosen.

Pausing before texting

One of the hardest but most powerful shifts for anxious partners is learning to pause before acting on the urge to reach out. When you feel the impulse to text, call, or seek reassurance, try giving yourself a small window first:

- Take a few breaths.
- Notice what you're feeling.
- Ask yourself, *What do I need right now?*

In today's world, most people have experienced some version of this desire for an immediate response. You may stare at your phone, waiting for a response and feeling your mind start to fill in the blanks.

EXAMPLE

Remy notices that Ava hasn't responded to his text in a few hours. At first, tells himself that Ava is just busy, but as more time passes, his thoughts start to spiral: *Did I do something wrong? Why hasn't she answered?*

Remy feels the urge to send another message, but he pauses instead. He takes a few breaths and notices what is coming up for him. He feels uncertain and anxious, something that's happened in past relationships. He calls a friend to distract himself, and he goes for a run. Rather than reacting, he gives himself a little time. He reminds himself that he doesn't have all of the information. After about a half an hour, Remy feels more settled.

TIP

Chapter 12 covers emotional regulation or lowering the intensity of your emotions. Pausing gives you the space to respond instead of reacting. Even a short pause can:

- Reduce the intensity of your emotions
- Help you communicate more clearly
- Prevent issues of overpursuing and reassurance seeking

Practicing tolerating uncertainty

Uncertainty is one of the most uncomfortable experiences for an anxious attachment system. The mind wants answers immediately.

Part of building security is increasing your ability to tolerate *not knowing*.

Here are some ways you can build that tolerance:

- Give yourself a reminder: *I don't have all the information yet.*
- Consider alternative explanations: *They might just be busy.*
- Let time pass before assuming the worst such as, "I just reached out a few minutes ago. I don't need to assume something bad has happened."

REMEMBER

Over time, you'll build emotional resilience to the discomfort of uncertainty.

When you're feeling uncertain, your mind will often try to fill in the gaps. You might notice yourself replaying conversations, checking your phone repeatedly, or looking for clues about what's going on. While these habits are very common, they tend to keep the anxiety going rather than settling it.

Here are some tools to help you with sitting with uncertainty:

- **Name the urge you're feeling:** *I want to reach out right now.*
- **Reality check your thoughts:** *What do I actually know for sure right now?*
- **Set a short window:** Give yourself 10 to 20 minutes before reacting.
- **Ground yourself in the present and use your coping skills:** Try telling yourself these things:
  - *I can take good care of myself right now.*
  - *I can sit with this feeling.*
  - *I can call a friend/go for a run/take a walk.*

TIP

Grounding yourself in the present can help settle your nervous system when your mind is jumping ahead. This might look like focusing on what's in front of you, taking a walk, or engaging your senses. Healthy distraction, such as watching show, finishing a task or talking with a friend is a great way to give your mind a break and lower the intensity.

Respecting your partner's need for space

When you're feeling anxious, your instinct is often to move closer. You may want to talk things through, get reassurance, or feel connected again as quickly as possible. When your partner is overwhelmed, their instinct may be the opposite. They may need distance, quiet, or time alone to calm their body and collect their thoughts.

This is where couples often get stuck in a painful loop.

The more one person reaches for connection, the more the other pulls away. And the more one person pulls away, the more urgent the need for connection becomes.

REMEMBER

Respecting your partner's need for space doesn't mean your needs don't matter. It means recognizing that space can support connection when it's handled clearly and intentionally.

You can express your needs without escalating the situation. You can tell your partner, *I feel anxious when we disconnect, but I understand you need some time. Can we check back in later?*

TIP

This kind of response does two things at once:

- It honors your feelings.
- It reduces pressure on your partner.

REMEMBER

When your partner feels less pressured, they're more likely to return to the conversation in a calmer and more present way.

Why space can help (instead of hurt)

Taking space isn't about avoiding the issue. It's about preventing the conversation from getting worse.

REMEMBER

When emotions are high, nervous systems can become flooded. In that state of heightened emotion, it's much harder to listen, problem-solve, or respond with care. Without a pause, conversations often turn into criticism, defensiveness, or shutdown.

A short break can allow both people to:

- Calm their bodies
- Organize their thoughts
- Return with more clarity and less reactivity

The key is that space should feel temporary and safe rather than permanent and unsafe, as abandonment often does.

EXAMPLE

Abe and Kristi have been dating for a year. One Friday night, something upsetting happens, and Abe brings it up the next evening. Kristi quickly becomes overwhelmed and asks for a break. She leaves the house to go for a walk. As soon as she leaves, Abe's anxiety spikes. His thoughts start racing: What if she's pulling away? What if this means something is really wrong?

He struggles with the distance and begins calling and texting her. When she doesn't respond, his anxiety grows even stronger. Meanwhile, Kristi feels flooded and emotionally overwhelmed. From her perspective, Abe isn't respecting her need for space.

The more Abe reaches out, the more Kristi wants distance. The more Kristi pulls away, the more anxious Abe feels.

This situation can shift with small but important changes.

EXAMPLE

> Abe could say, "I'm feeling anxious, but I'm going to give you space. Can we reconnect in 30 minutes?"
>
> Kristi could say, "I need a break, but I will come back and talk."

TIP

It's helpful for couples to have an understanding that when they take a break, they will return to the conversation. Research shows that most people need at least 30 minutes to settle their nervous systems. However, each person is different. I encourage couples to decide together (before they have conflict) what amount of time they usually need to return to baseline. That way, they have an understanding that they will revisit the topic within a certain time period, depending on their nervous systems and their collective needs. In particular, people with anxious systems do better when they know the timeframe.

These kinds of statements turn space int something predictable and reassuring, rather than something that feels like rejection or disconnection.

Resisting counterproductive behaviors

TIP

Respecting space also means resisting the urge to:

- Repeatedly text or call
- Demand immediate answers
- Check for reassurance in ways that escalate the situation

These behaviors are often born out of anxiety, but they're counterproductive because they tend to push your partner further away.

REMEMBER

Figuring out how tolerate temporary uncertainty is part of building a more secure connection.

IN THIS CHAPTER

» Noticing how attachment shows up

» Pacing connection

» Deciding whether to speak up or observe

Chapter 20
Dating with Attachment in Mind

Dating has a way of bringing attachment patterns to the surface quickly. You might find yourself thinking about someone you just met more than you expected, checking your phone more often, or questioning what their behavior means. Even when things are going well, there can be an undercurrent of uncertainty: *Where is this going? Do they like me as much as I like them?*

Early dating is full of unknowns, and uncertainty is one of the biggest triggers for the attachment system. When you don't have a shared history yet, your brain starts filling in the gaps. If you tend to lean anxious, you may look for reassurance and signs of consistency. If you lean more avoidant, you may feel the urge to slow things down or create space before things get too close. These responses are protective. But without awareness, they can shape how a relationship unfolds before it even has a chance to develop naturally.

In this chapter, I describe how attachment styles can shape the dating experience and influence the way you interpret uncertainty and connection to help you discover how to approach dating with greater self-awareness.

Spotting Attachment Patterns Early

REMEMBER

One of the benefits of understanding attachment is that you begin to notice patterns sooner. This helps you to understand what you're experiencing.

In early dating, attachment may show up in one of the following ways:

- » One person wanting frequent communication while the other prefers more space
- » Strong chemistry paired with inconsistency
- » Feeling deeply connected one day and unsure the next
- » A tendency to move very quickly or hold back emotionally

It can be tempting to label these moments right away: *They're avoidant* or *I'm being too much*. Instead of jumping to conclusions, try being curious. Use curiosity to ask yourself questions. Is this a one-time occurrence or a recurring pattern? Have I communicated my needs clearly? Secure dating does require that you tolerate some uncertainty while allowing enough time for patterns to reveal themselves.

Pacing the Relationship

Pacing is one of the most important and often overlooked parts of dating. When relationships move too quickly, attachment systems can become activated before you've had time to gather enough information about the other person.

TIP

When attachment gets activated, there can be a strong pull to either move closer quickly or create distance. But healthy relationships tend to build at a pace that allows both people to stay regulated and engaged.

If you tend to lean anxious, the following strategies may help you keep a new relationship on an appropriate pace:

- » Letting the relationship unfold instead of trying to define it early
- » Resisting the urge to text too much or overexplain
- » Giving the other person space to move toward you

If you tend to lean avoidant, pacing may mean:

- Staying present even when closeness increases
- Following through on plans instead of pulling back
- Allowing emotional connection to build gradually

REMEMBER

Pacing is about creating enough space for the relationship to develop without being driven entirely by fear or urgency.

Deciding When to Speak Up

One of the hardest parts of early dating is figuring out when to speak up about what you're feeling or noticing and when to give things more time. A common question in early dating is, "Should I say something or am I overreacting?"

Not every uncomfortable feeling needs to be addressed immediately. Sometimes, what you're feeling is part of getting to know someone new. Other times, sharing your feelings or observations can provide important information about the relationship and whether the other person is able and willing to respond to your needs.

TIP

Ask yourself this helpful question: *Am I reacting to a pattern or a single moment?* The answer can guide whether you share what you're feeling or sit with it a while.

It can also be a good idea to check in with a trusted friend, a therapist, or someone who knows you well and may also know your attachment tendencies. They can sometimes help you to figure out whether you're responding to a genuine concern, making assumptions, or reacting from past experiences that are being activated in the present.

It may be useful to speak up when:

- You're noticing a pattern rather than something that is a one-time occurrence.
- You can express yourself clearly rather than from a heightened emotional state.

For example, maybe communication has become less consistent, plans have started feeling one-sided, or you're noticing a change in the level of connection. Rather than assuming the worst or staying silent, you might say, "Hey, things have felt different lately. Can we check in about how you're feeling?"

Identifying red flags versus attachment activation

Determining whether a situation is a case of attachment activation or is a true red flag in a relationship is one of the areas where many people get stuck. In this section, I provide some guidance to help you determine the difference.

Attachment activation can feel intense. It can make you question, worry, or second-guess what's happening. But you should neither think that every uncomfortable feeling is a sign that something is wrong, nor should you dismiss every concern as "just your attachment style." It's useful to distinguish between red flags and attachment activation.

Part of dating with awareness is learning to tell the difference. Here are some signs you may be dealing with attachment activation:

- You notice familiar fears showing up (rejection, abandonment, being trapped).
- Your reaction feels bigger than the situation.
- You feel an urgency to act quickly (text, pull away, seek reassurance).
- You notice that you're scanning for danger.
- You notice that you're filling in gaps with worse case assumptions.
- You're focusing on flaws to create distance.
- You're feeling overwhelmed by closeness or expectations.

Asking questions to help you sort it out

When you're feeling uncertain, it can be difficult to know whether you're responding to a genuine concern, an attachment trigger, or a combination of both. Rather than rushing to conclusions, try slowing down and gathering more information. The following questions can help evaluate patterns, assess compatibility, and decide whether what you're experiencing reflects a relationship concern or an activated attachment system.

- **Communication and contact**
  - Do they respond in a way that feels generally consistent over time?
  - When there are gaps in communication, do they acknowledge them or ignore them?

- Do you feel like you're always the one reaching out or initiating?
- Do they respect space?

» **Addressing difficult topics**

- When you bring something up, do they stay engaged or shut down, deflect, or disappear?
- Do you feel heard, or do you leave conversations feeling dismissed or brushed off?
- Are they able to tolerate a little discomfort in order to work through something?
- Are they able to respect needs for conversation breaks or incapacity to talk?

» **Consistency**

- Do their actions generally match what they say?
- Do they follow through on plans or frequently cancel or change things at the last minute?
- Does the connection feel steady or unpredictable?

» **Ownership and accountability**

- Can they acknowledge when they've hurt you?
- Are they able to say "I can see how that affected you" without becoming defensive?
- Do they take responsibility or tend to shift blame?

» **Safety and trust**

- Do you feel like you can be yourself around them?
- Do you feel more grounded or more anxious and unsure after spending time together?
- Over time, does your sense of trust grow, or does it feel shaky?

6 The Part of Tens

IN THIS PART . . .

Discover ten key principles of attachment theory.

Become familiar with ten attachment-based affirmations.

Find out ten ways to self-soothe when you're in attachment activation.

IN THIS CHAPTER

» Knowing why people are wired for connection

» Understanding how attachment influences relationships and communication

» Moving toward greater security

Chapter 21

Ten Key Principles of Attachment Theory

Attachment theory can feel complex when you're first diving in to it. This chapter pulls together the most important ideas into ten core principles you can keep in mind as you notice attachment playing out in your everyday relationships.

You're Wired for Connection

Humans are biologically wired to seek connection with others. From infancy through adulthood, our nervous systems are shaped by relationships. Wanting closeness, reassurance, and emotional safety isn't a weakness. It's how we're built.

REMEMBER

Attachment theory starts with this simple truth: Connection is a survival need.

The reason this matters is that many people grow up believing they should be more independent, less sensitive, or less needy. Attachment theory reframes connection not as dependency but as biological drive that supports resilience, regulation, and well-being across the lifespan.

Attachment Patterns Start Early

Your earliest relationships teach you what to expect from others when you're distressed, vulnerable, or in need of comfort. These early experiences don't determine your future, but they do create a starting point.

Attachment is shaped less by single events and more by repeated emotional experiences over time and what was consistent, unpredictable, welcomed, or discouraged.

REMEMBER

Exploring early attachment is not about deciding whether your childhood was good or bad or assigning blame to parents or caregivers. Most parents do the best they can with what they have. Attachment theory focuses on patterns, not blame.

There Are Four Main Attachment Styles

Attachment theory commonly describes four patterns:

- Secure
- Anxious
- Avoidant
- Disorganized

WARNING

These are not labels or diagnoses. They're descriptions of patterns that can show up differently across relationships and life stages. Many people recognize parts of themselves in more than one style.

REMEMBER

Attachment styles are best understood as tendencies under stress. They aren't fixed identities. You may feel secure in one relationship and activated in another based on context and history.

Attachment Needs Are Normal

Wanting reassurance, closeness, responsiveness, or emotional presence does not make you "too much." These are normal attachment needs shared by all humans. Problems arise not because needs exist, but because needs are mismatched, misunderstood, or unmet.

People often struggle more with how needs are expressed than with the needs themselves. Attachment work helps people learn to recognize needs earlier, before they come out as protest, withdrawal, or conflict.

Stress Activates Your Attachment System

You may feel calm, flexible, and confident in relationships until stress hits. Illness, loss, transitions, conflict, or exhaustion can all activate your attachment system. Under stress, attachment patterns become more visible.

REMEMBER

People often think "I thought I'd worked through this already." In reality, stress narrows your window of tolerance and brings attachment needs closer to the surface.

Partners Trigger Each Other's Patterns

In close relationships, attachment is interactive. One person's anxiety can trigger another person's withdrawal. One person's distancing can trigger another person's pursuit. This creates cycles that feel personal but are often predictable and patterned. Understanding these dynamics helps shift the focus from blame to awareness.

REMEMBER

Most relationship distress is within a cycle, not in one person alone.

Repair Is More Important than Perfection

No relationship stays perfectly attuned. Misunderstandings, missed signals, and hurt feelings are inevitable. What matters most is repair — the ability to come back, acknowledge impact, and reconnect. Secure attachment is built not by avoiding rupture but by repairing it.

REMEMBER

Repair can be acknowledging hurt, clarifying intent, moving toward your partner, or returning to a conversation after cooling down. Small, consistent repairs matter more than grand gestures.

Coregulation Builds Safety

You don't figure out how to regulate emotions alone. We acquire the skill through relationships by being soothed, understood, and responded to. Over time, repeated experiences of coregulation help you develop internal regulation. Safety grows with awareness and new responses.

TIP

Even as adults, nervous systems respond to tone, timing, and responsiveness.

Attachment Drives Intimacy and Communication

Attachment shapes how you express needs, handle conflict, and interpret your partner's behavior. Many communication problems are actually attachment problems in disguise. Understanding attachment helps explain why certain conversations feel loaded, repetitive, or emotionally charged.

REMEMBER

When communication feels stuck, the underlying question is often: "Am I safe? Do I matter? Will you be there for me?" Try to reframe how you perceive your response to a situation to figure out what is prompting it.

Change Is Possible

Attachment patterns are learned, and what you learn can be adjusted. With awareness, supportive relationships, and intentional practice, people can develop earned secure attachment. Your past influences you, but it does not define you.

REMEMBER

Researchers use the term *earned secure attachment* to describe people who didn't grow up with secure attachment but developed greater security later in life. Through self-awareness, supportive relationships, therapy, and repeated experiences of safety and responsiveness, people can learn new ways of relating to themselves and others.

REMEMBER

Change doesn't require perfection. It grows through repeated experiences of safety, responsiveness, and repair over time.

IN THIS CHAPTER

» Strengthening your relationship with yourself

» Building safer and more secure connections with others

» Practicing beliefs that support secure attachment

Chapter 22

Ten Attachment-Based Affirmations

Affirmations aren't about pretending everything feels easy or repeating words until problems disappear. In attachment work, affirmations are best understood as gentle reminders, ways of offering your nervous system a new, steadier message over time. You don't have to believe every affirmation right away. You only have to be willing to practice them, especially in moments when old attachment patterns are activated.

I Am Worthy of Love and Connection

Your ability to be loved does not depend on being perfect, fixing everyone's problems, or always being independent. You exist, and that alone makes you worthy.

Why this matters: Many people internalize messages that they are "too much" or "not enough." Repeating this affirmation that you deserve love no matter what reminds your nervous system that you don't have to earn love. It's your birthright.

Example: After experiencing a conflict with a friend, you remind yourself that being imperfect does not make you unworthy of love or belonging. Instead of assuming you will be rejected, you allow yourself to remain open to connection.

It's Safe for Me to Express My Needs and Feelings

Needs are not burdens. They are information about your inner world. Expressing them honestly is a healthy part of any relationship.

Why this matters: When needs are ignored or suppressed, anxiety or withdrawal often shows up later. This affirmation trains you to feel safe expressing yourself before patterns escalate.

Example: Telling your partner, "There is something that has been bothering me. Are you available to talk?"

I Am Learning to Soothe and Regulate My Emotions

Emotional regulation is a skill, not a trait you're born with. It's something that gets better with practice, and each moment of awareness is progress.

Why this matters: Attachment wounds don't disappear overnight. This affirmation emphasizes self-compassion and practice, not perfection.

Example: Taking three slow breaths before responding to a triggering text or journaling feelings instead of immediately reacting.

I Can Be Close to Others without Losing Myself

Closeness does not require losing yourself. You can maintain autonomy while being vulnerable and connected. This is possible.

Why this matters: People with anxious or avoidant patterns often confuse closeness with enmeshment or loss of independence. Repeating this affirmation helps shift that belief.

Example: You can say yes to a dinner invitation while keeping a personal hobby or boundary intact.

I Can Honor Others' Needs while Caring for My Own

Balance is key. Relationships thrive when both parties' — yours and your partner's — needs are considered.

Why this matters: Many people default to caretaking or withdrawal to manage discomfort in relationships. This affirmation reminds you that mutual care is possible.

Example: Checking in with a friend about their day and then taking time to recharge yourself afterward.

I Can Tolerate Temporary Uncertainty and Remain Connected

Not every discomfort signals danger. Some ambiguity is normal and tolerable.

Why this matters: Uncertainty often triggers anxious attachment patterns. Practicing this affirmation strengthens your ability to stay present without spiraling.

Example: Waiting to hear back from a friend before assuming they're upset or abandoning you.

Every Day, I Practice Being Present, Open, and Emotionally Available

Security grows through consistent small moments.

Why this matters: Even small, repeated efforts to be attentive and present build trust and nervous-system safety over time.

Example: Listening fully during a conversation, putting your phone down, or checking in about feelings.

I'm Developing Awareness about Myself and Others

Awareness is the foundation of change. Each time you notice a reaction, pattern, or emotional shift, you're building capacity for secure connection.

Why this matters: Understanding triggers and attachment patterns gives you new choices.

Example: Noticing that you feel anxious when a friend cancels plans and choosing to breathe instead of sending a panicked text.

I Am Capable of Building Safe and Secure Connections

Your past does not dictate your future. With insight, supportive relationships, and intentional practice, you can create connections that feel steadier, safer, and more responsive.

Why this matters: Attachment theory shows that earned security is possible. We can change patterns.

Example: Investing in a friendship or romantic relationship where boundaries and responsiveness are honored.

I Can Build Relationships Where I Feel Seen, Heard, and Valued

Healthy connections allow your thoughts, feelings, and experiences to matter. This affirmation embodies the core goal of attachment work: feeling recognized, understood, and respected.

Why this matters: People with insecure attachment histories often learn to hide parts of themselves, assume their needs don't matter, or fear that being fully known will lead to rejection. This affirmation reminds you that healthy relationships make room for your thoughts, feelings, and needs.

Example: Sharing an idea, expressing a desire, or asking for feedback without shrinking or overexplaining.

IN THIS CHAPTER

» Using self-soothing strategies to calm your nervous system and regain perspective

» Responding to distress with grounding, self-compassion and healthy coping strategies

Chapter 23

Ten Ways to Self-Soothe When You're in Attachment Activation

When your attachment system gets activated, your body reacts. Your heart speeds up, your thoughts get louder, and everything can start to feel urgent, overwhelming, or even threatening.

Self-soothing isn't about ignoring your feelings or pretending you don't care. It's about helping your nervous system settle enough so you can respond instead of react.

Here are ten ways to steady yourself when your attachment system is on high alert.

Name What You're Feeling

Before you try to fix anything, slow down and label what's happening inside you.

You might say to yourself,

- "I'm feeling anxious right now."
- "This feels like fear of being rejected."
- "I think I'm getting triggered."

Naming your emotion helps your brain shift out of panic mode and into awareness.

Remind Yourself, "I Don't Have All the Information"

Attachment activation often fills in the blanks with worst-case scenarios.

Try grounding yourself by saying things like this:

- "There could be other explanations."
- "I don't know the full story yet."

These ideas create just enough space to stop your mind from running too far ahead.

Slow Your Breathing

Your breath is one of the fastest ways to calm your body.

Try this: Inhale for a count of three. Hold your breath for a count of four. Exhale for a count of seven.

Longer exhales signal safety to your nervous system. Even a minute or two can make a noticeable difference.

Put the Phone Down

If you're activated, your urge might be to text, call, check, or recheck. Instead, give yourself a pause:

- Set a timer for 10 to 20 minutes
- Step away from your phone

Ground Yourself in the Present

When you're triggered, your mind often goes to the past or jumps into the future. Try grounding yourself in the present by doing one simple task.

Pick something simple: wash dishes, respond to an email, sort clothes, step outside, sweep the floor. Let yourself be fully in that moment instead of in your thoughts about what might happen next.

Move Your Body

Activation builds energy in your system. Movement helps release it. Find some activity that gets you up and moving:

- Take a brisk walk
- Stretch
- Shake out your arms and legs

Use Your Senses to Soothe

Your senses can help regulate you quickly.

You might:

- Wrap up in a soft blanket
- Take a warm shower
- Hold a hot mug of tea
- Smell something calming like lavender

These small sensory cues signal comfort and safety.

Speak to Yourself with Compassion

In moments of activation, your inner voice can get harsh or panicked. Try shifting it so that it's speaking to you in a kinder way:

- "This is hard, but I can handle it."
- "It makes sense I feel this way."
- "I'm okay, even if this feels uncomfortable."

You're not trying to convince yourself everything is perfect, but you're offering yourself steadiness.

Delay Big Conversations

When you're highly activated, it's harder to communicate clearly.

It's okay to say, "I want to talk about this, but I need a little time to settle first."

TIP

Coming back to the conversation later often leads to a better outcome and fewer regrets.

Reach for Safe Connection

Self-soothing doesn't always mean you have to do it alone. You can reach out to others to give you a hand.

If you need support, consider:

- Calling a trusted friend
- Talking to a therapist
- Sitting near someone who gives you a sense of being grounded

The goal is connection that calms not connection that escalates the situation.

Index

Numerics

A

B

C

D

E

F

I

J

K

L

M

N

P

R

S

T

U

V

W

About the Author

Kelley Lockhart Delaune, LCSW, is a licensed clinical social worker, couples therapist, and owner of Modern Therapy & Wellness, a group therapy practice in New Orleans, Louisiana. She specializes in couples therapy, attachment, and relationship health. She specializes in working with couples in couples' weekend intensive sessions. Kelley integrates attachment theory with evidence-based approaches to help clients navigate communication, conflict, trust, and emotional connection. In addition to her clinical work, she provides workshops, writes educational content, and trains professionals on relationship and attachment topics. She is passionate about helping people to heal their relationships with themselves and others. She believes that all humans can grow and change.

Author's Acknowledgment

First, thank you to the team at Wiley and the *For Dummies* series for the opportunity to write this book. A special thank you to my editor, Charlotte Kughen, whose thoughtful feedback helped strengthen these chapters. Thank you as well to Tracy, Nina, and everyone who worked behind the scenes to bring this project to life.

To my mentor, Debra Voelker, LCSW, thank you for your wisdom, guidance, and unwavering support over the years. Your influence can be found throughout my work and in the clinician I have become.

Thank you to Elizabeth Earnshaw, LMFT, for your encouragement, friendship, and generosity. I am deeply grateful for your support and for the many ways you have encouraged both my work and my growth.

While the examples in this book are fictionalized to protect privacy, they are inspired by the themes that emerge every day in the therapy room. To the many clients who have trusted me with their stories, thank you. It is a privilege to do this work alongside you.

Finally, to my parents and my husband, thank you for your love, encouragement, and support throughout my life. Your belief in me has made so many opportunities possible.

Dedication

To my husband, children, and parents. Thank you for being my secure base.

Publisher's Acknowledgments

Acquisitions Editor: Tracy Boggier
Project Editor: Charlotte Kughen
Managing Editor: Ajith Kumar
Production Editor: Magesh Elangovan
Cover Image: ActionGP/stock.adobe.com